"For more than a decade the Chicago Bears have held their annual Summer Training Camp at Olivet Nazarene University. During that time I have had the privilege of getting to know Dr. John Bowling, the university president. I have watched how he has led the school in a long, steady climb to prominence, with increased enrollment, campus expansion, added quality, and an enhanced reputation. In this new book, *ReVision*, Dr. Bowling shares some of the strategies that have guided the success of the university for more than twenty years. The application of these principles can help extend the effectiveness of any leader. It's a great read!

Brian J. McCaskey,
Senior Director of Business Development
Chicago Bears Football Club

"As a university president, John Bowling has demonstrated extraordinary leadership over an extended period of time with integrity, authenticity, creativity, core values, and perseverance. He is a master at telling stories that will inspire you. In his book entitled *ReVision* he has identified strategies and lessons learned that will help any leader in any organization create a legacy that can be an example for future generations. Read it and practice the strategies to renew your work, your organization, and your life."

Robert L. Sloan,
CEO of Sibley Memorial Hospital in Washington, DC

"John Bowling is clearly a thoughtful, successful leader. Not all such leaders have both the willingness and the talent to share the lessons they've learned. But thankfully, John does. In this book the content is rich, and the writing is engaging. John is a master of insightful analogies and a teller of good stories, both of which are great tools for effective teaching — and open doors for enjoyable learning. Get your pens and highlighters ready."

Brad R. Moore,
President of Hallmark Hall of Fame Productions

REVIS ION:

RE VIS ION:

JOHN C. BOWLING

ReVision: 13 Strategies to Renew
Your Work, Your Organization, and Your Life

BEACON HILL PRESS
OF KANSAS CITY

ISBN 978-0-8341-2943-6

Printed in the
United States of America

Cover Design: Arthur Cherry
Inside Design: Sharon Page

10 9 8 7 6 5 4 3 2 1

CONTENTS

PREFACE

*Genuine beginnings begin within us, even when they are
brought to our attention by external opportunities.*

—William Bridges

This book has been written in the context of my work during the
past twenty-two years as a university president. Looking back
across the twists and turns of that administrative landscape, I see
a set of strategies that have served me well. They have allowed
me to renew my work, my organization, and my life at various
points along the way. These strategies, along with a set of lessons
learned, inform each page of this book.

Because I write about what I know best, there are several refer-
ences to higher education in general and my work at Olivet Nazarene University in particular. However, the scope and application
of the strategies discussed here are broader than the field of higher
education. These strategies have nearly universal application.

In addition to reflecting on my own work, I have sought input
from leaders in various other fields. Those encounters reinforced
my realization that in whatever field we work, in the final analysis one does not lead a business, organization, or university—one
leads people. Therefore, the focus of this book is primarily on the
strategies that help a leader, particularly one who serves in one
location over a long period of time, to continually and effectively

relate to and motivate the men and women with whom he or she works. In doing so, a leader can renew his or her work, organization, and life.

Over the past two decades the university where I work has tripled enrollment, raised its academic profile, expanded the campus, added several major buildings, and ventured into international, on-line, and distance education, all the while staying focused on its mission and core constituents. Across the years with the growth of the university, the variety of technological advances, and shifting cultural norms and expectations, the leadership challenges have changed as the university has moved through various chapters in its development. It has been my privilege, in the midst of these crosscurrents of culture, business, and education, to provide leadership for the university and to grow and develop as a person and a leader.

CONTEXT

I first came to Olivet Nazarene University when I was fifteen years old. It was the equivalent of what the university now calls "Red Carpet Days"—a few days set aside each fall for high school students to visit the campus to see what it might be like to attend Olivet. Until that time I had no personal connection with Olivet and very little understanding of higher education at all. My parents didn't attend college. My older brother had just enrolled at Houghton College, a Wesleyan school in upstate New York, but he and I had not talked much about what college was really like. Perhaps the thing that drew me to Olivet on that first occasion was simply the chance to get out of high school for a day or two.

I still have several vivid memories of that journey. I made the trip by car with a few other high school students from our area. Our driver was a pastor from a neighboring community. We left about four o'clock in the afternoon and drove on two-lane roads all the way from my hometown in western Ohio to Bourbonnais, Illinois.

In those years there was no formal campus entrance. In fact, most of the university was hidden from view behind a row of old houses on the main street of Bourbonnais. So as we got close to the school, our driver turned into a residential neighborhood several blocks south of campus, and we drove the remaining distance on Bresee Avenue.

The first thing I noticed on the campus was the smokestack—"ONC": Olivet Nazarene College. Then in the foreground I saw a large, stately looking church and beside it an area filled with barracks-type buildings that were known as "GI-ville." This was army surplus housing from World War II that was being used for married students.

Our meals that weekend were in the Miller Dining Room, and I slept for the next few nights on a cot in the basement of the nearest church—College Church. Little did I know—how could I have known?—that less than twenty years later I would serve as the senior pastor to that congregation and put other people to sleep while they listened to a sermon.

I had a good time on that first visit, but I didn't go away with a sense of destiny or clarity. I didn't say to myself, *This is where I am going to school.* But it was a start, and sure enough, when I finished high school a few years later, I chose Olivet. Harold W. Reed, a distinguished leader, was president, and the campus was in the midst of a major development plan that included the incredible feat of constructing ten buildings in ten years.

I started as a business major my freshman year, but during the summer between my sophomore and junior years, I sensed a clear call to ministry and changed my major to religion. During those years I began to date a wonderful girl named Jill, who was from

Ohio as well. We were married the summer after I graduated, and I enrolled that fall in the master of arts program at Olivet.

A year later, with my course work finished, we packed everything we owned into a handful of boxes, put them in the backseat of our 1968 VW Beetle, and headed for Fort Worth, Texas, for graduate school. I remember pulling away from campus, thankful for my Olivet experience, and assuming that my formal association with ONC was over and that I would be back only occasionally as an alumnus returning for homecoming festivities or stopping to visit the campus if I was in the area.

We lived in Texas for the next four years and loved every minute. One summer while we were living there, we drove back to the Midwest to see our families in Ohio, and on our return trip to Texas we stopped by Olivet. We drove on to campus late on a Friday afternoon and pulled up in front of Burke Administration Building. Jill said, "Let's go in and see if anybody is around."

As we were walking in, President Harold Reed was walking out. We stopped to visit with him for a few minutes, during which time he told us that it was his last day as president of Olivet. It was a poignant moment. We had a rather personal conversation with "our" college president as he looked back on more than a quarter century of service to Olivet. There was certainly no way we could have known that one day I would move into the corner office he was vacating that day.

Two years later, Jill and I moved from Texas to Colorado Springs, where I had been invited to join the faculty at Nazarene Bible College. Near the end of that first year, I returned one day to my faculty office to find a note on my desk: "Please call Dr. Sayes, Olivet College." That phone call led to an interview and an offer to teach at Olivet. So we packed up again and moved east from Colorado to the Olivet campus.

We arrived during the first week of August and moved into Williams Hall, where Jill had agreed to serve as resident director to the freshman women. I had spent quite a bit of time in Williams Hall as a student but had never really thought about living there. It turned out to be a great experience.

However, Jill soon discovered that being a resident director was not a job but rather a way of life. It was front-line ministry, but the rewards were terrific. Jill did an outstanding job and still keeps in touch with many of those "girls" today. Those were busy years—I taught in the religion division, Jill worked in student development, and we both felt much fulfilled.

However, before long I received a call inviting me to serve as senior pastor of the First Church of the Nazarene in Dallas. Soon we were packing and driving away from campus once more, assuming that our formal association with Olivet was ending for sure this time. Our days in Dallas were rich and rewarding.

Then one evening four years later I received a call to return to the Olivet community as the senior pastor of College Church. So we packed our things and headed back, yet again, to ONC.

For the next eight years I served the church, the campus, and the community as pastor. In the spring of 1991, while I was still at College Church, Leslie Parrott, president of Olivet at the time, announced his retirement. In mid-July the board of trustees came to campus for a farewell dinner for Dr. and Mrs. Parrott and to meet later that evening for the purpose of electing a new president.

Jill and I attended the farewell dinner. Years earlier we had just happened into Burke Administration Building on the last day of Dr. Reed's presidency, and now we were there for Dr. Parrott's farewell as well. At the time, we were living just across the street from the Olivet campus in a house that is now the alumni center.

Following the dinner we returned home, assuming we would learn the name of the next president of Olivet the following morning.

About 1:15 AM our phone rang. I was sound asleep. When I answered the phone, the secretary in the university president's office said, "Dr. Bowling, the chairman of the board of trustees would like to talk to you."

Now? "Okay," I said, still half asleep and standing in the dark. Board of Trustees Chairman B. G. Wiggs greeted me with these words: "Dr. Bowling, I am calling to let you know that you have just been elected the twelfth president of Olivet Nazarene University. Congratulations! Can you come to the administration building to meet the Board?" Suddenly I was wide awake.

I dressed hurriedly, looked in the mirror, and discovered that in the night my hair had divided into teams and gone off in different directions. I combed it quickly and then walked across the street to meet—my future.

After talking briefly with the board, I returned home, where Jill and I sat up the rest of the night trying to process what had just happened. The following evening we were in Springfield, Illinois, where I was giving a speech for Olivet at the Illinois District Assembly of the Church of the Nazarene.

A NEW PRESIDENT FOR OLIVET

Fast-forward eighteen years to the summer of 2009, the last week of June, in Orlando, Florida, where the General Assembly of the Church of the Nazarene was being held. Delegates from around the world were there to transact the business of the international church. I had been elected to the general superintendency of the church four years earlier at the General Assembly in June 2005 and had declined the election—so I wasn't too worried about having to face that decision again.

However, much to my surprise, I was once more elected as general superintendent. After a few hours of consideration, I accepted the position but almost immediately felt checked and uneasy. Although I was greatly honored and humbled by the vote of the assembly, the following day I rescinded my decision and declined the election once more.

On the way back to Olivet from Orlando, Jill and I began to play the "what if" game. What if I had not rescinded my decision? Saying yes to the election would mean we would soon be packing our things and moving away from Olivet as we had done before. Then, within a reasonable timeframe, the Board of Trustees would have come to campus again, just as they had in 1991, to elect a new president.

Our "what if" discussion got me thinking about what it would be like for the new president of ONU. A new president of Olivet would arrive with fresh eyes and new energies. A new president would not take anything for granted. He or she would survey the landscape, evaluate the strengths and weakness of the university, and listen carefully to the counsel of faculty, students, staff, alumni, and the board to determine the priorities and direction for his or her leadership.

A change of presidential leadership can be a traumatic time, but it can also be a time of renewal and refocus for an institution. After thinking about this for a while, I decided the time was right for me to become the "new" president of Olivet Nazarene University—to start again, to begin anew, and to look at Olivet with fresh eyes as best I could.

As I looked back, it was clear that the years had been productive and happy years and that the university had shown strong progress in nearly every aspect of our work. But I also began to realize that if Olivet were to be all it could and should be in the days to come, our dreams for the future would have to outweigh our memories of the past.

I wanted to do more than simply rewind the tape and assume that the next years were to be a repeat, or even a continuation, of the past. I was not interested in business as usual, because I believed that Olivet was an "unusual" place, and we had an unusual opportunity for continued growth and development. From this experience came the opportunity to begin again and thus to re-vision my work, my organization, and my life.

Across the years the world has changed, the school has changed, the environment for higher education has undergone dramatic changes, and I have changed as well. How does one continue to provide effective leadership in the same place over a long period of time, particularly in an environment of nearly unprecedented change? It is that question that gave rise to this book.

By carefully analyzing my experience and talking with many others who have served businesses, schools, churches, and organizations over time, I determined there are certain strategies to effectively re-visioning one's work, organization, and life. My hope is that this book can help extend the service and increase the effectiveness of others who are called upon to provide leadership to organizations for extended periods of time.

INTRODUCTION

*When you feel you have reached the end and that you cannot go one step
further, when life seems to be drained of all purpose—what a wonderful
opportunity to start all over again, to turn over a new page.*
—Eileen Caddy

*Nobody can go back and start a new beginning,
but anyone can start today and make a new ending.*
—Maria Robinson

Several years ago Jill and I were living in Dallas, where I was
pastoring a wonderful church. We came home late one evening,
and as we walked to the front door I asked, "May I use your keys?"

"I didn't bring my keys," she said.

"I thought I had mine, but I can't seem to find them," I replied.

I checked once more in the car, but no keys. It was late, it was
dark, it was cold for Dallas—and there we stood locked out of our
own home.

"It could be worse," I said. "It could be raining." Sure enough,
just then a light rain began to fall.

I walked around to the back of the house; that door was secure. I began to try the windows. After a few minutes of casing
the joint, I returned to the front porch, where Jill was waiting
patiently, tucked in out of the rain.

"I have good news and bad news," I said. "I found an open
window."

"Great," she replied. "What's the bad news?"

"It's too small for me."

I pushed the window open as far as it would go, and I pulled together a couple of things for Jill to stand on. Just as she was about halfway in, I heard my neighbor yelling out his back door, "What's going on over there?" He had evidently seen people moving around our house in the dark.

I hated to tell him that I had forgotten my keys and that I was now making my wife climb through the window in the rain, so rather than going into all of that, I called back, "Hey—it's me, John. I locked myself out, but I think I've got everything under control. Thanks."

Just then I heard Jill hit the floor inside and mumble something about "What do you mean *you've* got everything under control?"

It is very frustrating to be locked out, to be standing at the door but unable to enter. It is exasperating, because the real purpose of a door is not to keep people out—it is to let people in.

Just so, across the landscape of long-term leadership, one encounters a series of doors—some seem to swing open automatically and lead to new opportunities for growth and development. At other times, leaders find themselves standing in front of a door without the proper key to unlock the next chapter of personal and organizational development.

The keys that are needed for effective long-term leadership reside in a set of strategies, each of which helps individuals see new possibilities that are often hidden in plain sight. These can provide added energy and possibilities for leadership in the same place over a long period of time.

The strategies that follow provide a set of lenses through which leaders can take a fresh look back, a renewed look within, and an optimistic look ahead. Leadership need not be—cannot be—doing the same things in the same ways year after year. Leaders who serve the same organization for a long period of time must find moments in which to take a careful look back in order to stay in touch with the founding vision of the organization and with the unique nature of the organization they lead. This look back is a process involving the following four steps: *remember, reevaluate, restore,* and *resolve.*

Søren Kierkegaard, the nineteenth-century Danish philosopher, once noted that life must be lived forward but can be understood only backward. This is true for institutions as well as individuals. Thus, this look back is a centering exercise that in turn can become a vital part of one's evaluation of the present needs of a business or organization. In the process of re-visioning, leaders must also look within to re-engage, repair, release, and refresh those areas of the organization and those of his or her professional life that may have become dormant or ineffective. These four steps mark a beginning again and carry with them the seeds of a new beginning for both the leader and the business or organization served.

Too often managers manage for yesterday's conditions, because yesterday is where they got their experience and had their successes. But management, and particularly leadership, is about tomorrow, not yesterday. The focus is on what should be done rather than what has been done. Because a leader must always have an eye on the horizon, there must also be institutional and personal moments to look to the future. Going forward, one must lead and facilitate a reticulation, where needed, and offer a re-articulation of the organization's shared vision, values, and goals. He or she will need to resist the pull of the past and the power of the status quo to bring genuine renewal to his or her work, organization, and life.

WANT TO BUY A RUG?

A few of years ago I was speaking at a leadership conference in the coastal city of Antalya, Turkey. Following the conference, Jill and I stayed on for a brief tour of the archeological sites in western Turkey. One afternoon while returning from a site, we stopped at a small workshop where a team of talented craftspeople were weaving beautiful rugs.

During our visit we watched the production of fine threads of wool, cotton, and silk. We viewed the dying process, which produced both muted and brilliant colors. We observed artists developing intricate patterns and designs. Then we stood for a long time watching a young woman operating an ancient loom. Strand by strand, she wove the threads together. Through the work of her nimble fingers and strong grip, a rug began to appear. It was durable, useful, and most of all—it was beautiful.

The secret to the beauty and permanence of such rugs rests in the fact that the various threads are "interwoven." As I studied the process, three things struck me.

First, it was very clear that a single thread alone could not compare in strength or splendor to a thousand threads woven together in harmony with a grand design. The ordinary became extraordinary as the threads began to intertwine.

Second, it was obvious that handmade rugs take time. There is no automated processes involved, no time clocks to punch—just the slow, steady pace of one thread following another. Little by little, strand by strand, hour after hour, the work continues. I was reminded that things of beauty and things that last take time.

Third, I noticed that one had to stand on the proper side of the process to see the beauty. If one watches the weaving from the back side, he or she sees only a jumble of colors and textures; there is no pattern, no meaning, no real beauty. Only as one looks at the pattern from the perspective of the person who is doing the weaving does the process begin to take shape.

What is true of fine rugs is true of our work, our organizations, and life itself. There are many strands—individually each has value and meaning, but the greater value rests in the sum of the parts. Building and sustaining a business or organization is a similar undertaking. There are many strands that need to be interwoven to enhance the beauty and usefulness of each and to collectively create a thing of lasting value. Leaders have before them a bundle of threads: opportunity, human resources, technology, financial assets, intellectual capital, latent or evident product or service demand, and the opportunity to create something that will have significantly more value and meaning than the mere sum of the parts.

There are moments over the course of time when organizations, like fine rugs, may need renewal or repair to extend their life, beauty, and usefulness. How does one renew his or her leadership over time?

Leadership in the same place over a long period of time brings its own set of challenges. As the world, the business environment, and the people with whom and for whom one works changes, so must the leader. Jack Welch, former CEO of General Electric, said that effective leadership is the ability to change the tires on a car as it's moving down the highway. The capacity to revision one's leadership in the midst of the demands of the day is an essential skill if an individual is to engender the possibility of long-term effective service and significance.

I like the observation made years ago by United States Secretary of State John Foster Dulles, who said, "The measure of success is not whether you have a tough problem to deal with, but whether it's the same problem you had last year."[1] It is alarmingly easy for leaders and their organizations to find themselves caught in a revolving door—lots of movement but no real progress—for they just keep coming back to the same issues.

An effective leader develops the capacity to use each challenge and problem as a doorway to the next level of effectiveness, for as problems are faced and resolved, new opportunities arise. Every day, several times a day, we enter rooms through the simple act of walking through a doorway. We do so without thinking about it. We just know, intuitively, that to enter a room we must go through the doorway.

This act of entering through a doorway is a fine metaphor for leadership. Choosing the right doors and moving through those doorways opens new business and leadership possibilities. Too often we stay in the same room, doing the same kinds of things, not knowing the vast array of possibilities that wait for us in the next room. There are a set of strategies that have been time-tested by professionals in all avenues of leadership. These strategies provide a set of keys that can unlock new opportunities and possibilities.

SECTION 1
THE LOOK BACK

1
RE
MEMBER

In the dim background of our mind, we know what we ought to be doing, but somehow we cannot start.

—William James

Don't look further for answers: be the solution. You were born with everything you need to know. Make a promise to stop getting in the way of the blessing that you are. Take a deep breath, remember to have fun, and begin.

—Jonathan H. Ellerby

The first strategy for long-term effective leadership in the same place is to *remember*. Over time, memories fade, one's thinking gets cluttered, and in the midst of inevitable cycles of change leaders can lose touch with the "center" of themselves and their organizations. When that happens, work becomes a rote exercise—just showing up, doing what has always been done, rewinding the tape each morning but without the passion, purpose, or compelling vision that inspires and energizes an organization. If an individual is to genuinely revision his or her work, he or she must remember the most important and essential core elements of the organization and of his or her role in the life of the organization. Institutional and personal memories are powerful forces when harnessed to a new vision.

When Howard Schultz, the founding president of Starbucks, returned to the position of CEO in an effort to save the company from a corporate decline, he noted, "Sometimes the earliest days of Starbucks seemed very far away. Like straining to remember the sound of your child's voice as a toddler as he or she heads off to college, Starbucks' nascent days got more elusive as the company grew."[1]

ARE YOU THE SINGER?

Several years ago I was asked to speak for a weekend series of services at a church in western Michigan. The music for that weekend was provided by a very fine trio of musicians—a fellow and two young ladies from a neighboring town. The meeting began with a Friday evening service, and I thought we got off to a good start. There was a large crowd in attendance, and the music was excellent. At the close of the service, I had the opportunity to greet a large number of folks from that congregation who had come to the service.

As I was standing in the foyer, a man walked up to me and asked, "Are you the singer?"

"No, I'm the speaker for the weekend."

"Where ya from?"

"Olivet Nazarene University."

"Oh, I had a boy went there. He never came back."

"Hum," I replied, not knowing what to say to that.

"Do you know where Niles is?" he asked.

"Well, more or less," I said. "I've never been there, but I know in a general way where it is."

"I have a brother who lives there," he said.

The conversation trailed on a bit longer until another person walked up to say hello.

The following night we had another service. The trio sang; then I spoke. I lingered in the foyer to greet the people. The same fellow came up to me once again.

"Are you the singer?" he asked. As you can see, I was making quite an impression on this guy. I had spoken twice for twenty or thirty minutes each night, and he couldn't tell the difference between me and the nice young man doing the music.

"No," I replied. "I'm the speaker."

"Where ya from?" he said.

"Olivet Nazarene University."

"Oh, I had a boy went there. He never came back."

"Hum," I replied, still not knowing what to say to that.

"Do you know where Niles is?" he asked.

"Well, more or less," I said.

"I have a brother who lives there," he said.

The next morning, Sunday morning, I came to church and spoke once more and then that night, the closing night of this brief weekend meeting. I arrived a little early for the service and was seated in the pastor's study collecting my thoughts. After a few moments, I heard the door open gently. I looked up expecting to see the pastor, who had stepped out earlier, but instead, there stood the man with whom I had talked the two nights before.

He, too, must have expected to see the pastor, for he seemed quite surprised to see me. He stared at me for a moment and, shaking his finger, said, "Are you the singer?"

I said, "No. You might want to write this down—I'm the speaker."

"Where ya from?"

"Olivet"

"Oh, I had a boy went there—"

"Did he ever came back?" I asked.

"No, never came back," he said.

"Do you know where Niles is?" he asked.

"Yes, I think your brother lives there, doesn't he?"

"That's right, I have a brother who lives there," he said.

That experience was somewhat humorous and sad at the same time. I'm sure this individual was a wonderful gentleman whose memory had simply become impaired. It could happen to any of us.

Memory is a wonderful thing. It is upon our ability to remember that all learning rests. It is the capacity to recall that allows us to function beyond a mere stimulus-response level. Take away a person's memory, and you take away a great deal of what it means to be a person. Such is the tragedy of Alzheimer's disease and other forms of senility.

To remember gives us—

the ability to relive days gone by,

to recapture special moments in life,

to recall friends and family from a former day.

Memory can be stimulated by the will or by the moment. Have you had the experience of hearing a song and through that music a door of memory is opened and you recall an event when that song was playing?

TWENTY-SEVEN YEARS IN THE HOSPITAL

Robert L. Sloan spent more than twenty-seven years in the hospital, not as a patient, fortunately, but as a hospital administrator. He is the former president and chief executive officer of Sibley Memorial Hospital in Washington, D.C. He is a fine example of a leader who provided fresh, innovative, and effective leadership to a complex organization over a long period of time.

Patients and staff often remark on the friendly, personal attitude that can be instantly felt at Sibley. It's a feeling that perfectly reflects the personality of the man at the hospital's helm since 1985: a president/CEO who drives employees to work when it snows, visits patients on Thanksgiving and Christmas, and is sending personal handwritten notes to hundreds of employees saying he's grateful to have worked with them. In describing Robert Sloan, certain words surface again and again: *ethical, visionary, honest, genuine, approachable, humble.*[2]

As noted, Bob began his tenure as president of Sibley in 1985. Across the years, in the midst of a constantly changing healthcare environment, he led Sibley to premier status. The hospital was recognized as the best community hospital in the Washington, D.C., metropolitan area by a survey of 1,500 physicians. In recognition of his sterling leadership qualities, the District of Columbia Hospital Association established the Robert L. Sloan Leadership Award, to be presented annually to an individual demonstrating leadership qualities inspired by Bob.

One important key of Bob's continued success was his keen sense of personal and institutional memory. Across the years he never forgot who he was (his values, work ethic, faith, commitments, and professional readiness) or what the primary mission of Sibley Hospital was. This act of remembering became a constant and continual source of renewal for both him and the hospital.

During his tenure of service, the physical footprint and scope of service for Sibley was dramatically increased through new facilities and services. Under his leadership the hospital averaged greater than six-percent net operating margin each year for twenty-seven years, and the hospital's balance sheet grew from $40 million in 1985 to $575 million in 2012, with nine hundred days of cash-on-hand. During this same period a variety of challenges were met, and a host of creative new programs were implemented.

Through it all, employee retention rate was ninety-seven percent, and morale throughout the organization remained high.

In early 2006 Bob began to talk of "the new Sibley." The final chapter of his service was characterized by a strong, compelling vision of what was yet to come for the hospital. He wasn't about to *coast* his way to retirement. He remembered clearly the passion and vision that had characterized his early years at Sibley, and he renewed his conviction that the best days for his institution ought to lie just ahead. This final phase of his legacy was marked by a formal integration with the prestigious Johns Hopkins Health System and the planning for the construction of a new primary patient care tower.

In April 2012 Bob was invited to address the Interagency Institute for Federal Health Care Executives. After providing an overview of his years of service at Sibley, Bob provided his eager audience with a list of lessons learned. The list represented not only lessons learned but also lessons remembered and practiced daily. These became the hallmarks of his leadership and gave him balance and buoyancy in the cross currents of leadership. Among the list were the following:[3]

Hiring the best people makes all the difference. Good qualifications and experience are important, but the best people have a positive, can-do attitude, perseverance, initiative, energy, enthusiasm, commitment, and dependability. Learn how to identify those characteristics and recruit accordingly, and in turn your organization will be more successful than you can ever imagine.

Treat people as you would be treated. Every member of the organization is important. What employees do on a daily basis will either help or harm the reputation, the effectiveness, and the financial stability of the organization.

Assign your best people to the biggest opportunities. There are many people within organizations who can handle problems; but generally there are only a few who can take advantage of the big opportunities. By identifying those people, identifying your opportunities, and matching the two together, the organization will move in a positive direction and achieve success that is meaningful.

Remember that good judgment is the most important attribute of the successful executive.

Be guided by a vision and a mission that is inspiring. Find the nobility in the endeavor, communicate it, challenge employees with it, and reach as high as you possibly can.

Create a sense of the significant. Leaders are constantly deciding among alternatives, such as how to spend one's time and resources. Identify what is essential to the organization, and spend your time working on those things.

Concentrate on revenue growth. Be creative, innovative, and flexible.

Control expenses, monitor productivity, enforce efficiency.

Emphasize quality, outcome measurement, and personalized service.

Learn from your mistakes. Making mistakes is both a humbling and healthy experience. Every leader makes them—the secret is to correct the mistakes and move on.

Remember that success comes not so much from big victories but little victories each day.

Make decisions. Trust your judgment, and be willing to commit yourself and stake your reputation on the results. This will cause you to consider carefully and think clearly.

Listen more than you talk. The greater function is not to answer questions but to ask them. This helps to define issues and involve others.

Seek continuous improvement. Good is never good enough. We can always do better.

Caution: success will make you more vulnerable to temptation than failure ever will. Be careful when you achieve success, because temptation is lurking nearby (ethical, moral, financial).

Find good in all situations.

Take time to reflect. Having quiet time will provide needed space to gain perspective, clarity, and strength.

Realize that a thank-you from the CEO means more than you can imagine. Bob noted, "After a successful joint commission survey, I sent a personal letter to each employee. The response was surprising. It meant more than all the free meals, the desserts, and the cookies combined. Also, a brief thank-you note to one employee per week or month will mean much."

Walk around; be visible. One almost always learns something while visiting with others in the organization. While making the rounds, be optimistic, have a sense of humor, and encourage others.

Maintain a constancy of purpose.

Respect the elderly. Talk to them, listen to them, and try to learn from them.

Keep in mind that change always takes more time than you expect.

Read a psalm or proverb daily. Psalms and Proverbs represent the wisdom of the ages. They will provide a perspective on life, a compass, a guide, a source of strength and encouragement.

Develop strong teams that will work together.

Finally, enjoy each day, for it is a gift.

Bob Sloan not only learned these lessons across the years, but he also remembered them, put them into practice, and passed them on to others.

Mr. Sloan's strong work ethic and down-to-earth attitude were shaped by an Indiana boyhood filled with chores, blue-collar jobs, family, and faith. It was while he was working his way through Olivet Nazarene College as an emergency orderly that he first heard of "hospital administration." After four years of distinguished service as a captain in the U.S. Army, including the command of a communications intercept detachment on the Thai/Cambodian border during the Vietnam War, he earned a graduate degree from George Washington University and began his career in hospital administration.[4]

To remember is a key strategy in the process of renewing one's work, organization, and life. "Every organization has a memory, a history of achievements, mistakes, and even unintended consequences that contribute to an ongoing dialogue as people mold an event's meaning for themselves. The tapestry of interpretations informs, and often directs, the organization's future."[5]

The "how" of remembering can and should take a variety of forms. Certainly there is the internal remembering that provides a constant backdrop for the thinking, reflection, and planning of the leader. But that is not enough. Remembering must also be a public exercise. Leaders must capitalize on moments when the narrative of an organization can be told and linked to the present. Strong leaders find ways to recall organizational heroes of the past.

In a recent President's Dinner speech to the faculty and staff, I devoted several paragraphs to tell the story of how during the first few years after my election as president of Olivet I had the privilege of talking at length on several occasions with Harold Reed, who served as Olivet's president for twenty-six years, from 1949 to 1975. In the course of those conversations, he provided good, godly counsel, and he gave me several mementos of his tenure at Olivet.

One of the things he gave me was a framed three-word saying that was on the wall of his office during his years as president. It says simply, "God Is Able." In a way, that says it all, doesn't it? We don't know what the future holds, but we can have the assurance that God will enable us to respond to whatever obstacles or opportunities may come.

He also gave me his presidential medallion, which had been presented to him by the alumni association on the occasion of his inauguration in 1949. Putting that medallion on, I said, "Most of you know I have a new medallion, commissioned by the Board of Trustees during our Centennial Celebration. It is very fancy, with the names of all the former presidents engraved on it. But this one, the one I am wearing, is even more special, for it links me to the great heritage of our past and reminds me that someone else will wear it after my term of service has ended. It is a symbol of the stewardship of this office." All of this contributed to a moment of remembering.

On another occasion, in my opening remarks at the dedication of a new chapel on campus, I sought to connect that moment with both the mission of the university and those who had gone before us, saying,

> Good morning and welcome. We gather in a spirit of celebration and thanksgiving to dedicate the Betty and Kenneth Hawkins Centennial Chapel and the Crawford Auditorium.
>
> May the steel and stone of this structure bear witness to the mission of Olivet Nazarene University. Let the cross at the top of centennial tower, one hundred feet high, cast its shadow on those who live, work, and study on this campus and on all who pass by.

May the grass, trees, and flowers of these grounds speak in colorful chords of wonder and praise for the God of creation, and let the mirrored dome of heaven be a canopy of grace and blessing both day and night.

Our university "Alma Mater" says in part, "The time we spent within these halls will ne'er forgotten be." Therefore, let us remember. Let us remember those who have gone before us, giving more than a century of service to Olivet.

We give thanks for individuals with names like Nesbitt, Richards, Willingham, Larsen, Reed, Chalfant, Gibson, Galloway, Snowbarger, Sayes, Mitten, Kelley, Parrott—a handful whose names recall hundreds of others whose sacrifice and service have brought us to this glad hour. Most are now unsung and unremembered, yet they are known and numbered among a great cloud of witnesses who join us today from heaven.

Thus, we celebrate and give thanks for more than a building. We celebrate the faithfulness of God, and we give thanks for the faith, faithfulness, and generosity of God's people.

Simply saying, "Let us remember" begins to call to mind images and individuals who help center a present moment into the timeline of the continuing story of an organization.

When we established the ONU China Initiative and began offering courses in Hong Kong, a ceremony was held in the Benner Library and Learning Resource Center. Placed on permanent display was a large antique replica of a Chinese merchant ship of centuries ago. That large wooden model is still on display in the library as a constant reminder of the university's connection with China. In the stairwell leading to the classrooms and laboratories of our Family and Consumer Science Department hangs a beautiful and valuable Chinese garment, displayed in a handsome wood case. It, too, is a reminder of our China Initiative. Articles such as these and other visible reminders—building names, donor recognitions, trophies, and photos—all call the campus to remember who we are and from where we have come.

Special days throughout the academic year such as Homecoming, Scholars Week, Commencement, Grandparents Day, Founders Week, and so on are public occasions for remembering. The idea is to consciously and consistently keep the past alive— not as a shrine or even as a template to be repeated, but just as one measures direction by the wake of the boat, the past can provide a needed reminder of where one has been and thus provide a sense of direction and/or correction for the future.

An effective leader must always remember the guiding vision that gave birth to an organization that provides the overarching trajectory for its future and then be able to remind others of this vision. Robert Townsend writes, "Vision grabs. Initially it grabs the leaders, and through their enthusiasm, followers and other stakeholders start paying attention."[6]

Commenting on what it means to have a vision and keep that vision alive over time, Warren Bennis tells of talking with the leader of a major medical school and hospital with a huge budget and hundreds of employees who summed up his job in a single sentence: "I spend most of my time reminding people of what's important."[7]

A clear and steady institutional memory helps keep things stable as the environment in which an organization exists changes. It is disconcerting to realize that forty percent of the companies that appeared on the Fortune 500 list ten years ago are no longer there. A prolonged recession, along with a cycle of mergers, acquisitions, leveraged buyouts, increased global competition, and a myriad of other factors, has changed the landscape. To navigate such choppy waters a leader must be guided by an internal compass as well as the stars above. That compass must point unerringly toward the mission of the organization, thus providing a clear sense of why the company or organization exists.

It is easy for one to lose single-mindedness over time. Even a slight variation in emphasis or corporate direction can lead an organization away from its core competencies, and before long, secondary interests and issues become the central focus. A leader's primary responsibility is to guard the mission and guide the organization with a steady hand while at the same time foster innovation and change.

This is what Noel Tichy and Mary Anne Devanna called transformational leadership. Their classic book *The Transformational Leader*, written a generation ago, continues to ring true, for its principles are timeless.

> Transformational leadership is change, innovation, and entrepreneurship. . . . These are not the provinces of lonely, half-mad individuals with flashes of genius. Rather, this brand of leadership is a behavioral process capable of being learned and managed. It's a leadership process that is systematic, consisting of purposeful and organized search for changes, systematic analysis, and the capacity to move resources from areas of lessor importance to greater productivity. . . . It is a discipline with a set of predictable steps.[8]

It is particularly important for those individuals who serve in senior leadership roles for a long period of time with the same organization to be able to initiate and sustain a culture and process of transformation. I continue to be amazed at the twin dynamics at work in my organization between a much-needed continuity one year to the next and the clear recognition that each academic year is, in fact, new. Higher education, like health care and business in general, continues to change, and unless a leader can change along with this process, he or she will soon cease to be effective.

The core competency needed is for leaders and their organizations to change without changing. "A challenge in leadership is to accept and manage change without altering what is vital to the health of an organization. In the midst of change . . . leaders hold on to and preserve the heart and essence of an organization's identity." Resistance to change, along with the opportunities change brings, creates a certain dynamic tension that must be managed. "Change can be a genuine opportunity for renewal, but the problem is that change has no constituency."[9]

If the university does not change and adapt to new waves of technology and changes in pedagogy and curriculum design, and if it cannot accommodate the shifting desires of students related to housing, food service, recreation, and extra-curricular activities, it will soon find itself swimming upstream rather than riding the currents. Yet if a school or any other organization forfeits its core identity and values in search of the latest market trends, it, too, will find itself in the backwaters with nothing to distinguish itself from a crowded field.

In an interview/dialogue between the founding CEO of Southwest Airlines, Herb Kelleher, and the present Southwest CEO, Gary Kelly, Kelly was asked, "You've made a number of significant changes at Southwest Airlines since you became the chief executive officer. Change, we both understand, is necessary for long-term survival. But do you have a perception of what has *not* changed about Southwest Airlines?" Kelly's answer is instructive. He replied that it was the core values that had not changed and that it was those values, perhaps even more than the changes made, that ensured the long-term viability of Southwest.[10]

Robert Sloan at Sibley Hospital was able to strike the perfect balance of change and consistency. In a way, one could make the case that Bob and his leadership team transformed the hospital and its related enterprises by keeping it the same. Their commitment to mission and consistent patient care, coupled with an aggressive posture related to medical technology and physician needs, along with sensitivity to the constantly evolving medical and healthcare fields, enabled the hospital not only to survive during Mr. Sloan's long tenure of service but also to thrive.

One of the observations I made in the book *Grace-Full Leadership* was that an effective leader focuses on the body, not the head. That means that the measure of one's leadership, particularly over time, is not seen in how well the leader is doing personally or professionally but on how well the organization is doing. I recently noted a celebration for a university president's twenty years of service in which he was lauded for his strong and effective leadership. It was all very nice, but what was not said or seemingly not recognized was that after two decades at the helm, the school's enrollment was stagnant and actually lower than it was two decades before. The school's financial performance was marginal at best, and its overall reputation had not changed. It seemed, from a distance, that there was little more to celebrate than the mere passage of time.

To avoid having little more than longevity as the hallmark of one's leadership, effective leaders must look for and sometimes create opportunities to re-vision an organization so that it can adapt to new challenges and opportunities. This re-visioning begins with a look back to remember and reconnect with one's core identity and ongoing story, which in turn provides a starting point to begin the process of moving forward.

2
RE
EVALUATE

There will be a time when you believe everything is finished.
That will be the beginning.
—Louis L'Amour

The beginning of knowledge is the discovery
of something we do not understand.
—Frank Herbert

Gratitude is a form of wisdom. It is patient, loving, hopeful, and rigorously
honest. It denies nothing, and it overlooks nothing. It looks reality full in
the face and says: This is true, this is me, this is my situation, and I have the
opportunity to build from here. This is my starting point, and I will succeed!
—Phil Humbert

Marshall Goldsmith has written an intriguing book. The title nearly says it all: *What Got You Here Won't Get You There: How Successful People Become Even More Successful!*[1] At one point he talks about how successful leaders often suffer the same set of self-delusions that golfers sometimes face. For example, he suggests that just as golfers when evaluating how well they play will often focus on the one or two great shots made in the course of a round—and overlook the scores of other shots that fell short or wide of the mark—they think they are doing better than they really are.

This propensity to overestimate one's success and overlook one's weaknesses can keep an individual from getting better over time. To counter this tendency, the effective leader learns to reevaluate both the nature of his or her leadership and the health and productivity of one's organization. Goldsmith writes that his book will have met its desired end "if I can help you consider the possibility that, despite your demonstrable success . . . you might not be as good as you think you are."[2] Successful leaders, facing those areas or their work and lives that need improvement, learn the lesson of reevaluation.

UP FROM THE ASHES

About fifteen years ago one of my young relatives announced his college choice to the family. He declared, "I'm going to Elon College, in Elon, North Carolina." I was embarrassed to say that although I had been a college president for nearly a decade by that time, I had never heard of Elon. However, that was soon to change, and not just because a relative was enrolling there as a student. It also happened that a dramatic, revolutionary change at Elon was just starting to garner national attention.

One spring break, my wife and I took a driving trip to the southeast United States, looking at colleges with the particular purpose of evaluating various admissions facilities. We visited Vanderbilt, Wake Forest, the University of North Carolina at Charlotte, and several smaller schools along the way. Our trip ended with a visit to Elon, not so much to see the school but to visit with our young relative. I immediately recognized two important things. First, I could see and sense that Elon was one of the best-kept secrets in higher education, and second, it was clear that a transformation was underway.

After that first visit, I soon returned to Elon with two of our vice-presidents. We met with the senior staff and began to analyze the principles at work in this obvious reevaluation and subsequent re-visioning of Elon. Since then, I have sent other teams of staff and administrators (admissions, development, and facilities management teams) to visit Elon in order for them to observe the changes underway there.

Today the transformation that has taken place there is truly remarkable. For the 2011-12 academic year, Elon's enrollment was five thousand nine hundred sixteen students. The campus is comprised of six hundred acres and a score of fine new buildings and the fifty-six-acre Elon University Forest, a land preserve and natural area for scientific research.

On its web site, the university notes that

Elon sends more undergraduate students to study abroad than any other master's-level school in the nation, and was named one of the top three universities in the nation for community service by the federal government's Corporation for National and Community Service. In addition, seventy-nine percent of students complete internships, forty-five percent of students hold at least one campus leadership position, and about 375 students work annually with faculty members on undergraduate research projects.

Elon students come from forty-eight states, the District of Columbia, and fifty-seven other nations. But it hasn't always been that way.

Four decades ago Elon College in north central North Carolina was described . . . by one North Carolina scholar as "a small, unattractive, parochial bottom-feeder," struggling to fill its freshman class and pay its bills. Today Elon University is a beautiful, medium-size university attracting students from forty-eight states with a new library, student center, science facilities, football stadium, and fitness center. Parents, visitors, and students often come away from the country club-like campus with something approaching awe. College guidebooks now list it among the three hundred finest undergraduate institutions in the land.[3]

Elon was founded in 1889 and had some modest success in the early years, never gaining much attention outside of its home territory of Alamance County, North Carolina. When Leo Edgar Smith became president of Elon in 1931, its enrollment had dwindled to just eighty-seven students, and the handful of faculty had not been paid for nearly a year. Dr. Smith went to work sending five hundred letters to area residents asking for donations to save the school. He received two replies with gifts totaling $13. He broadened his appeal to alumni and churches and finally raised enough to open the college for the fall term of 1932. George Keller writes, "President Smith spent most of the 1930s eluding creditors, borrowing money, and recruiting students."[4]

By the end of the decade, Elon's enrollment had grown to a respectable six hundred sixty students. However, with the onset of World War II, enrollment fell once more. By sheer determination, Dr. Smith held the school together during the war years, and then with the help of the G.I. Bill, new students returned to Elon in sufficient numbers to reestablish some measure of stability. When he retired in 1957, in his seventies, Dr. Smith had raised enrollment to one thousands six hundred students.

Upon President Smith's retirement, the board of Elon elected a young chemist, James Earl Danieley, to serve as president. He was just thirty-two years of age and had been serving as a member of the Elon faculty for a few years. He turned his attention to strengthening the academic profile of the school, expanding the library, and constructing several academic buildings. In 1973, when he left the presidency to return to the classroom as a teacher, enrollment stood at eighteen hundred students. Most of those students were still local, and many were not well prepared for serious academic work.

RE-EVALUATION BEGINS

The seeds that would later yield a harvest of change for Elon were planted in 1973 with the election of a new president, J. Fred Young. Like his predecessor, Dr. Young was young, just thirty-eight years old. Nonetheless, he was already known as an excellent educational administrator, having served as assistant superintendent of schools in Burlington, North Carolina, and deputy superintendent of schools for the commonwealth of Virginia. He had a doctorate from Columbia Teachers College in New York.

His first task was to re-evaluate the school's strengths and weaknesses. He realized their financial situation was precarious. They had a small endowment, modest fundraising success, and ninety percent of their revenue came from student tuition and fees. Enrollment was therefore critical.

President Young's evaluation revealed two notable factors related to enrollment. First, more than ninety percent of the students came from North Carolina and Virginia, and second, most of Elon's students were average or below average students from families of modest means. He also noted that in little more than a decade the state of North Carolina had opened fifty new community colleges, including one not far from Elon. This change in the educational landscape posed a serious problem for Elon, whose tuition was five times the cost of these new state-supported schools.

In addition to this new wave of educational alternatives for area students, President Young, drawing on his public school administrative experience, realized that the Baby Boom had reached its peak in 1961, which meant that college enrollments would peak by 1979. To make things even more challenging, Elon was only a short drive from the University of North Carolina at Chapel Hill and the rapidly growing, state-financed branch of UNC at Greensboro. "We thought we would lose students by the 1980s, so we had to scramble," Young says. The new president made admissions and the improvement of student life programs his first priorities.[5]

President Young remembers that "in those days fear was our great motivator."[6] The school was tuition-dependent and therefore had to concentrate on enrollment. Young and others believed that to increase enrollment, Elon needed to reevaluate its campus as it continued to improve academically and begin the hard work of broadening its development efforts.

To help lead this reevaluation and later revisioning of the Elon campus, a professional design firm was hired, which assigned a young visionary landscape architect, A. Wayne McBride Jr., to lead the process of creating the master plan for Elon's new campus. McBride went all out and presented a bold vision that was designed to create a park-like environment with a resort feel.

Keller writes, "When the faculty saw the drawings, they were thunderstruck and hung a huge sign that read, 'Welcome to Disneyland.'"[7] Young and at least a few of the trustees were taken back as well. Nonetheless, the board voted to approve the daring plan and launched a capital campaign to raise $5 million to underwrite the first phase.

While this visible, campus-wide facelift was underway, the more serious work of re-evaluating Elon's academic profile was also begun. The school applied for a two-million-dollar grant from the federal government's Advanced Institutional Development Program. To their modest surprise and elation, the college was notified in June 1977 that it had been awarded the grant. With that vital seed money in place, the Elon faculty and staff went to work transforming the inner workings of the school, just as a phalanx of bulldozers was transforming the appearance of the campus.

A learning resource center was established. Teams of faculty began to carefully revise the curriculum. A fine career planning and placement office was established, and gifted students were identified for special help to apply for professional and graduate school admission. All this renewed energy led to increased interest from alumni and friends. By 1979, the year when the demographic data indicated a natural drop in enrollment, the school had increased by thirty-eight percent. And that was just the beginning of a process that continues today.

President Young understood that leaders must find ways to align the dominant culture and ethos of an institution with the organization's various subcultures. One of the things that must be done as an organization undergoes a pervasive re-vision and renewal is a conscious development of subcultures to support the different aspects of the developmental process.

As we began to re-vision our future at Olivet, we realized that various components of the student experience would need to be improved and coordinated. This started with an enhanced subculture change within our undergraduate admissions department that focused on both the science and the art of recruitment. A strong customer-service orientation was coupled with a relentless attention to the metrics of the admissions process.

Added to the admissions renewal was an adjustment of our student development program. We already had a strong professional student development team in place; what was needed was clear communication and coordination with admissions to ensure a smooth enrollment, matriculation, and orientation for new students. It was important for us to ensure that promises made by the admissions staff would be embraced and implemented by the student development team. Financial aid and student accounts were other areas that were coordinated to a new model of customer service. Soon a genuine synergy developed, which continues to fuel growth and strong morale.

In addition to these improvements, we realized over time that the professional level of our Human Resources Department would need to be improved to help make sure that the right people were filling the right jobs and that an overall positive staff culture would be developed. "The human resource system can be a very powerful tool in making the cultural system congruent with the technical and political system."[8]

FOUR QUESTIONS

The need for senior administrators as well as middle managers, to live and lead in a constant state of reevaluation, cannot be stressed too much. The pace of change is such that what was fine and effective a year ago might very well be counterproductive today. Schools, businesses, and organizations must create a culture and set of systems that continually ask these four questions:

- What are we doing well?
- What are we doing that needs to be improved?
- What are we not doing at all that we ought to be doing?
- What are we doing that we need not continue?

Do not underestimate, or dismiss as naive, the power of these four very simple questions. They provide a way to garner honest feedback and define reality, not as one may wish it were or as it used to be—but as it is now. If leaders and those who work closely with them can and will create a culture of constructive questioning that in turn becomes part of the fabric of organizational life, a pattern and rhythm of positive re-evaluation will then begin to energize, refresh, and renew the daily work of individuals at all levels of the company.

In talking about his tenure as a board member of the Peter Drucker Foundation, Marshall Goldsmith writes, "Among the myriad wise things I have heard Peter Drucker say, the wisest was 'We spend a lot of time teaching leaders what to do. We don't spend enough time teaching leaders what to stop. Half the leaders I have met don't need to learn what to do. They need to learn what to stop.'"[9] All leaders have a to-do list—the good leaders who last and find ways to renew their organizations also develop, at least from time to time, a "to stop doing" list.

One of the first things I did years ago as a new university president was to enlist the help of a veteran president to assist me in conducting an audit of our academic programs. Dean Hubbard, then president of Northwest Missouri State University, graciously agreed to work with us. He served as president of the school from 1984 to 2009, longer than any other in the school's history. Although it was not publicly known, just prior to and during the first few years of his presidency, consideration was being given by state officials to close the school by merging it with Western Missouri University, just forty miles south.

Dr. Hubbard immediately began an aggressive plan to renew the school and set it on a pace toward prominence. Before long, it became evident that Northwest Missouri State not only should remain open but also had a bright future under President Hubbard's leadership. One of his early initiatives, at a time when personal computers were just coming into existence, was the creation of what he called, "The Electronic Campus."

Dr. Hubbard was an experienced administrator and a visionary leader who had a broad understanding of higher education and yet a personal connection and sensitivity to what I was facing, for he was a graduate of Andrews University in Berrien Springs, Michigan, a school much like Olivet, and had served as president of Union College in Nebraska.

Under his skilled tutelage we began a process of re-evaluation. At the heart of the process was the development of a matrix that tracked the majors, minors, credit hours, faculty loads, and so on for each academic program. Once that work was complete, a picture began to emerge as to what we were doing well, what needed to be improved, what programs should be considered for closing, and what programs were missing altogether. Also, a similar process was developed for athletic and extra-curricular activities at Olivet.

This process of formally re-evaluating our programs gave way to a new set of plans that included dropping a few nonperforming programs and activities and replacing them with a new initiative called The Olivet Nazarene University Agenda for Excellence. What would be a natural activity for a new administrator/CEO should be a process that is repeated from time to time across the spectrum of one's leadership history with a given organization. A process of re-evaluation provides an important lens through which to view the health and vitality of an organization.

I began to use a little phrase during those early years of our re-evaluation that I continue to use each time we begin a new round of program evaluation. I realize that often the very process of evaluation becomes personally uncomfortable or even threatening to those who have been giving leadership and life to a current program now marked for improvement. Therefore, as we begin the process, I express my genuine appreciation for the accomplishments to date and take time to recognize the hard work of those involved. Then, as we turn our attention to the future, I say, "Let's remember: you don't have to be sick to get better."

The end in mind for re-evaluation is not about the past—it is all about the *future*, the next step. Great artist Michelangelo has been quoted as saying, "The greater danger for most of us lies not in setting our aim too high and falling short, but in setting our aim too low, and achieving our mark."[10] Leaders who can genuinely re-vision and thus renew one's organization have taken time to walk through a process of at least four important steps.

STEP BY STEP

First, effective leaders must do the hard work of self-examination and personal evaluation to connect again with one's strengths and weaknesses. There are a variety of tests and leadership/personality inventories available to aid in this process. Many times leaders will seek processional evaluation and feedback from organizational and executive development specialists. And generally this process will also involve feedback from work associates.

This can be threatening for many leaders, yet it is an important part of the process of getting better and a mechanism for identifying one's blind spots. Most leaders know their strengths, which they often overemphasize, and their weaknesses, which are often underemphasized; what leaders too often don't know is what they don't know. Thus, self-assessment is a vital starting point. Re-evaluation must begin within. Leaders who go the distance are willing to ask—and to listen.

A second step in this re-evaluation process is to look carefully at the key players on the team to ensure that they are working together in a unified manner. Sometimes an organization's structure may need to be adjusted; other times it is personality issues or poor communication that erodes the effectiveness of individuals working together.

I grew up in a small Ohio town surrounded by scores of fine family farms. One of the highlights of the summer was to attend the Miami County Fair each August. In addition to the normal amusements, there was always a display of outstanding livestock. From time to time, among the animals on display would be teams of horses, such as those that would have been used for plowing in generations past. Chief among the sturdy work horses was a breed called the Belgian drafts.

These are amazing animals that often weigh a ton and have an enormous pulling capacity. One Belgian can pull twice its weight, two tons. But the amazing thing is that when these horses are paired together, their pulling strength is increased exponentially. Together they can pull not four tons, but six, seven, or eight tons. The pulling power is multiplied when they pull together. So it is with effective working groups within organizations—productivity is significantly increased when individuals work effectively together.

Reevaluation begins within the leader himself or herself and then expands to look carefully at key individuals. A third step is that one must ensure that the organizational control systems are generating the right information at the right time to provide solid information on the health of various aspects of the organization and to amplify the effectiveness of one's decisions. Good data is essential to the good health of any organization.

Throughout these three steps, an environmental scan—both internally and externally—should be made to evaluate what is changing or has changed that will have an impact on the effectiveness of the organization. Are there new opportunities or threats on the horizon?

Solid reevaluation will require various levels of simultaneous diagnosis: self-evaluation, team evaluations, solid data, and good organizational sonar and radar that allows one to see in and through the fog.

VALUE CLARIFICATION

At the twenty-year mark of my leadership at Olivet, I sensed the need to engage the entire campus and many of our constituents in a comprehensive review of our university values. In talking with the senior-level managers and later to the faculty and staff as a whole, the challenge to clarify our values as we entered a new chapter of institutional development was presented along with a strong overriding caveat: our values statement had to be more than words on paper. If we were to invest time and energy in this endeavor, the end result must be a living document that would shape the life, priorities, and plans of the university on a daily basis.

What are core values? They are the primary values, which transcend time and place. They form the glue holding the various parts and processes of an organization together. Values are those core commitments that are preserved regardless of what others do. They provide the foundation for an organization's work and conduct. Values are not the work itself or the strategies and processes needed to get the work done; they are those factors that produce the climate in which the work is done. Therefore, they must be authentic and consistent.

THE IMPORTANCE OF VALUES

Jill and I have a little lake house in southwest Michigan, about two-and-a-half hours from campus. Several few years ago I purchased a small sailboat and named it *College Business*. If you call and someone tells you that I'm out on college business, you'll understand.

When I first hit the water I was reminded of the three basic rules of boating:

Open side up,

Pointy end forward, and

Boats don't go on land.

Beyond this, I learned a few other things as well. As I began to learn to sail, I observed some parallels between sailing and leadership.

1. The rudder is significant. It is the rudder that determines the direction of the boat. In any organization, the rudder is the mission and values. These are the guiding principles that determine the heading and direction for the organization. Without a steady, confident hand on the rudder, the wind will push the boat to and fro. There may be movement, but the direction will be unclear. The leader's hand certainly guides the organization, but too often a leader assumes that it is his or her hand alone that is on the rudder. However, in the most effective and efficient organizations, steering is a partnership among all stakeholders, because mission must guide everyone's efforts.

2. The wind is of major importance. One can have a fine boat and a steady hand upon the rudder, but without the wind there is no power. Many crosscurrents of wind come to bear upon any organization: public opinion, government, demographics, cultural and financial trends, technology, and politics, to name just a few. Part of the job of any leader is to choose the right wind. This takes a measure of intuition, experience, and analysis of the various crosscurrents at work at any given time.

3. The set of the sail matters. On the wall in the lounge of one of our resident halls on campus is a carving and inscription placed there years ago by an art professor named Rockwell S. Brank. It is a carving of a sailboat at full wind, leaning to one side. The inscription says it all: "'Tis not the gale—'tis the set of the sail that determines which way you shall go." Experienced leaders develop the art of trimming the sails to the right position to maximize the effect of market trends and other environmental factors an organization may be facing.

4. The anchor is a must. Without an anchor, organizations—like boats—will drift. It is the anchor that holds a ship steady in the storm. One's core values and the values of the organization become the anchor that provides stability.

Sailing is a good hobby and a vivid metaphor. About the time I bought my boat, I read a delightful book titled *First You Have to Row a Little Boat*. The writer, Richard Bode, provides a commentary on life by telling about his experiences of learning to sail as a boy. The title comes from his first day on the water. An old sailor agreed to teach him how to sail. The only thing the sailor would let the boy do the first few days was row a little boat. Bode writes,

> I sat in the center of the dinghy, facing the stern, my destination somewhere behind me, a landfall I couldn't see. I had to judge where I was headed from where I had been, an acquired perception that has served me well—for the goals of my life, and especially my work, haven't always been visible points of light on a shore that looms in front of me. They are fixed in my imagination, shrouded and indistinct, and I detect them best when my eyes are closed. All too often I am forced to move toward them backward, like a boy in a rowboat, guiding myself by a cultivated inner sense of direction that tells me I am on course, tending toward the place I want to be. And so in time the rowboat and I became one and the same—like the archer and his bow or the artist and his paint. What I learned wasn't mastery over the elements; it was mastery over myself.[11]

Surely he is right; we must be able to see where we have been in order to chart our course for the future. We must develop an inner sense of direction that keeps us steady in the water. This sense of knowing is vital not only for sailing but also for living and leadership, and it is grounded in and flows from values.

How are values kept?

The values that comprise the core of an organization's DNA do not automatically transfer from the board room or the corner office to the daily life of the organization. Values must be intentionally communicated and embodied in the men and women who make up the organization. Values are kept by people.

Values are also preserved and reinforced by policies that express what an organization cares about and by the overall corporate or organizational culture that develops. Also, values are kept by communicating them intentionally during the interviewing, hiring, and orientation processes. In those settings they are taught, but it is in the daily life of the organization that its values are "caught" by modeling them and emphasizing them on a consistent basis.

BACK TO THE BEGINNING

Most of what an organization becomes is formed in its earliest days. Imagine someone deciding to build a huge factory. The land is bought, an architect and builder are hired, and financing is arranged, bringing the project to completion. The machinery is assembled, and the workforce is hired. Then the leader holds a company-wide meeting and asks, "What product should we manufacture? What is supposed to go out those double doors of the shipping department and onto the semi-trailers and railroad cars? Why was this factory built?"

Or picture someone who gets a group of world-class athletes together and enters into contracts to pay the athletes huge sums of money, coaches and assistance are hired, and a lease is secured on a great stadium. Everyone involved gathers together for a meeting, and the person who led the project asks, "Let's see now—what kind of sport should we play?"

One does not start a work and then move to mission. Individuals start with a mission and then shape the work and use the resources to accomplish the mission. Mission drives, not follows, a great work. A problem, however, can sometimes develop as people join a work already in progress and begin to function as part of the group without ever really owning the dream or envisioning the vision.

If you were hired in the midst of building the factory, for example, that might be all you do at first. It could be easy for you under those circumstances to become convinced that the work of that particular business is the building and the maintenance of the factory itself. It is dangerously easy for a "means" to become an end in itself.

It can be that way in all organizations. Because leaders and key managers are called upon to spend so much of their time and energy building and managing the organization, often those endeavors become ends in themselves. Therefore, it is important to pause occasionally to be reminded and to reconsider the organization's history and the undergirding values and commitments that shape the work.

THE PARADOX OF SUCCESS

A paradox lies in the fact that the very beliefs that helped individuals be successful can over time become barriers to one's *continued* success. Goldsmith writes about this delusional thinking, calling it "the paradox of success." He points out why and how the aspects of this way of thinking create a resistance to change and thus a loss of momentum and continued success.[12]

The first of these mistaken beliefs is that "I" have succeeded. This focus on "I" can lead individuals to overestimate their role in their success. This is a fine line, for one certainly needs self-confidence and optimism, but this must be balanced by a realistic evaluation of his or her failures as well as successes. "To successful people, past is always prologue—and the past is always rose-colored."[13]

A variation of this shows up as a second mistake leaders make from time to time: the belief, consciously or not, that they possess a special ability to succeed in the future solely because they have succeeded in the past. This belief is what causes the star player to want the ball when the game is on the line. Successful people believe they can succeed, and that makes perfect sense; the risk lies in believing that success will automatically follow previous successes.

Success is not automatic, nor is it guaranteed, even for those who have been successful in the past. Yet these twin ideas, "I have succeeded in the past" and "I can therefore succeed in the present," occasionally convince leaders that they *will* succeed in the future. This somewhat false assurance can cause leaders to attempt certain things—or too many things—that others more prudently might resist. Added to the ideas that we have the skills, the confidence, the motivation to succeed is the idea that we can simply choose to succeed and it will come to pass.

These patterns of thinking, which often reside within successful people, tend to create a certain superstition that can come into play as one leads over a long period of time.

Superstition is essentially a faulty view of cause and effect. It is like the baseball player who puts his or her shoes on the same way before each game and somehow believes—or wants to believe—that this pattern has a positive impact on the way he or she will perform. This type of superstition can keep a leader from changing his or her work habits or patterns of behavior to attain continued success. He or she simply doesn't want to give up that which has "worked" successfully in the past.

To counter this, a leader must learn to consistently reevaluate every aspect of his or her work. This process of reevaluation is done both formally and informally, both individually and as a group. Formally, evaluation can be done first by the numbers— enrollment, production, sales, and so on. Watch the numbers, read the reports, ask the second and third questions. Occasionally it is helpful for an organization to use external consultants hired to lead a formal process of re-evaluation. Professional meetings and journals can also provide helpful feedback.

Informally, leaders must be able to gage the mood of the organization. *Is there a spirit of optimism? What is the enthusiasm level?* What do you hear as you listen for the off-the-record comment? An attentive ear and a willingness to listen can provide feedback as to what may need to be reevaluated or at least better communicated.

The process of reevaluation is much like one's annual physical. A set of vital statistics is recorded and compared to the list from last year's visit. Then a conversation occurs. "How are you feeling?" "Have you noticed any changes in eating, sleeping, or in your ability to function throughout the day?" "Are you experiencing any unusual pain?" "How about stress?"

Little by little a picture of health or the pinpointing of a problem begins to emerge. In some ways no one likes to go to the doctor; yet it is a vital part of staying healthy, particularly over a long stretch of time. The annual checkup helps preserve life and identify areas of concern that can lead to a set of procedures and processes designed to restore one's health and vitality.

Re-visioning begins with a look back over your shoulder to see from where you have come, thus remembering the purpose of the journey and recalling the accomplishments and lessons learned. This gives way to a conscious reevaluation of the present health of the organization. Are we being true to our values, are we still energized by the work we do, and are we connected in meaningful ways to those with whom we work?

3

RE
STORE

Desire is the starting point of all achievement, not a hope, not a wish,
but a keen pulsating desire which transcends everything.
—Napoleon Hill

One of the personal and then institutional guiding truths of Fred Young, who engineered the transformation of Elon University, is the simple phrase "A fine-quality institution is never static."[1] Alvin Toffler, the futurist of a generation ago who authored *Future Shock* and *The Third Wave*, was asked on one occasion why more of his predictions about the future did not materialize. He said that he had simply underestimated the power of the status quo.

Even in the face of inevitable waves of change, there is the tendency to do nothing, to remain static. Leaders must resist that pull. They need always to be searching for ways to restore the organizations they lead. This often begins by restoring a proper self-image.

IDENTITY THEFT

When I was in college I was a victim of identity theft. Today identity theft is big business that involves computer files, credit card numbers, automated teller machines, the Internet, and so on. My case, however, was a little less sophisticated, and I had never heard the term "identity theft" back then. That is what it was, nonetheless.

It was during my freshman year. I was living in the freshman men's dorm with my roommate, Steve. In those days, the exterior doors of the residence halls were always open, and Steve and I never locked the door to our dorm room. It simplified life; we didn't have to worry about taking a key with us, and, after all, we were at a Christian university.

Our system of no locks/no keys worked well for a time. Then one evening my father called me and said, "I got a notice today that your bank account is overdrawn. What's going on?"

"I don't know, Dad—I haven't written any checks," I said.

"Well, something's wrong," he replied.

A few days later a letter arrived from my father; enclosed were several canceled checks bearing my signature, except it *wasn't* my signature. I went to my desk drawer and pulled out my checkbook. Everything seemed fine at first. But as I looked a little closer I noticed that several checks had been torn from the back of the packet of checks in my checkbook.

Someone was stealing checks, signing my name, and taking the money. Most of the checks were being cashed at the campus business center. There were still a few checks unaccounted for, so I talked with my resident director, and he sent word to the cashier in the business center that someone posing as me was cashing checks.

Within a week or so I determined that one of the fellows on the floor above me was probably the person responsible for the theft. I began to monitor his whereabouts and behavior. One night I walked upstairs to find a huge pizza party underway. I asked one of the guys, "What's the deal?"

He told me that Michael, the person I suspected of stealing my checks, had just ordered several large pizzas for the men at his end of the floor. "Wow," I said. "Where'd he get the money?"

"I don't know," the guy replied, shrugging. "I think he paid by check."

So I walked down the hall to say hello. Mike smiled and said, "Hey, John—you want some pizza?" I though, *Well as long as I'm paying for it, I might as well have some.*

After a few minutes and a couple of slices of pizza, I slipped downstairs to tell the resident director. Later that night, after securing a copy of the check from the pizza place, he confronted Mike. He confessed, said he was genuinely sorry, and promised to pay me back, which he did.

I didn't think much more about it until later in the semester when I stopped at the cashier's window in the business center to cash a check. The young woman looked at the check, then looked carefully at me, looked back at the check and back at me. Then she asked, "Are you *you*? Or are you the other guy?"

"I'm me," I said.

"Okay," she replied, and without asking for any further verification, she handed me the money.

That was years ago. Yet her question comes back to mind from time to time. Are you *you*, or are you the other guy? That is a good question for any organization to think about, because organizations and the individuals who lead and manage them can also be victims of identity theft in subtle ways.

The story of Steve Job's on again/off again relationship with Apple is a fascinating one. He founded the company, was fired, then a few years later returned to lead Apple to new heights. When he returned to Apple, he realized that the company had drifted from a tight, compulsive focus on innovative and highly designed products to a period where the focus was on mass production with little attention to cutting-edge engineering or product design. The identity of the company had been compromised by focusing on profits rather than products. Little by little, perhaps with the best intentions, Apple's identity had been stolen from within. The company's core culture had been hijacked.

George Weigel notes, "History is driven, over the long haul, by culture—by what men and women honor, cherish, and worship; by what societies deem to be true and good, and by the expressions they give to those convictions in language, literature, and the arts; by what individuals and societies are willing to stake their lives on."[2] He seems to suggest that in the end history is all about culture—the overarching values, traditions, and shared lives of individuals.

If that is true in a macro sense for nations, ethnic groups, and so on, it is also true in a micro sense for businesses and organizations. Every group has a culture and ethos that expresses in tangible ways the life of that organization. Therefore, the process to revision an organization must include a clear restoration of institutional life and culture.

HAVE YOU EVER DONE THIS BEFORE?

Several years ago Jill and I decided to restore an old house. The house was built in the early 1900s and was for many years one of the finest houses in the community. Through a varied set of circumstances, the house had sat empty for a number of years and was earmarked for demolition. We decided to try to save the house. After about nine months of initial work on the house, we moved in and continued the restoration process over the next eight years while living there. What an adventure!

As the process of restoration unfolded through several stages, I learned a set of lessons applicable for restoring vision and energy to nearly any undertaking.

1. Restoration begins with a vision-shaped decision. The restoration of the old house didn't begin with the first hammer blow or brush stroke of paint. It began when we caught a vision of what had been and what could once more be and decided to act on that vision.

2. Clear out the clutter! An early phase in the restoration process was the removal of layers of debris that had accumulated little by little across the years. There was clutter and dust and chipped paint and damaged wood everywhere we looked, so much so that the original design and splendor was hidden.

3. Once the clutter was gone, we began to give the place a good cleaning, and an evaluation of what needed attention was required. This led to the development of a plan for restoring the house to its former glory.

4. Restoration takes time and consistent effort. It was a daily process. One of John Maxwell's books is called *The 21 Irrefutable Laws of Leadership*. I suppose one could protest such a grand title. And upon review, one might also be inclined to add or subtract from such a list. Nonetheless, John Maxwell's book by that name became a *New York Times* best seller.

Of those twenty-one laws, the one that has often caught my attention as I have worked my way through the twists and turns of leadership is his third law, or principle, of leadership. He calls it "the law of process."[3] In short, it is this: "Leadership develops daily, not in a day." His point is that leadership is a process and that learning to lead is a process as well. Referring to our renovation efforts, friends and neighbors asked, "Have you done this before?" to which I would reply, "No one ever does this twice."

5. Some scars remained as a reminder of the past. Even when we had finished the process of restoration, there were still a few scars here and there: a pane of glass that could not be perfectly matched or a section of inlaid flooring that had to be taken up

because of water damage from a leaking register. However, we soon realized that these were the marks of a living house. Each nick bore witness to children and pets and an active family life lived out across many decades. The scars and marks of age gave the house a certain character that was appealing.

COKE OR PEPSI?

As one seeks to renew an organization, one of the features that must be firmly in place, both for renewal to take place and afterward for success and full staff engagement to continue, is to create, foster, and reward a culture of empowerment and personal responsibility. This often takes time to fully put into place, but the results are worth the work and the wait.

I love the story John G. Miller tells in his engaging little book *QBQ! The Question Behind the Question.* One day as he was hurrying across town, he stopped for a quick lunch at a restaurant he was trying for the first time. The place was crowded, and it seemed at first that the waiter for his section had not been informed that he was there. Noticing that he had not yet been served, a young waiter from the neighboring section stopped to ask, "Have you been served?" and then offered to take his order.

John said all he wanted was a salad and a dinner roll or two. When the young man asked him what he would like to drink, John replied, "Diet Coke, please."

"I'm so sorry, sir. All we serve are Pepsi products. Would Diet Pepsi be okay?"

After a brief pause, John replied, "No, thanks. I really do prefer Diet Coke. But it's okay—I'll just have water with lemon."

A few minutes later the waiter returned with the salad, rolls, and water. But then in just another moment the waiter appeared once more with a tall glass of ice and a twenty-ounce chilled bottle of Diet Coke. "Wow!" John replied with a somewhat puzzled look. "I didn't think you served Diet Coke."

"That's right—we don't," the young man replied. "But the convenience store next door does."

"Who paid for it?" John asked, still in a bit of shock.

"I did, sir. It wasn't that much."

Pressing a little further, John said, "You've been here all the time—how did you have time to run next door?"

Smiling back at him, the waiter said, "I didn't, sir. I sent my manager."[4]

That's empowerment. And it not only added to the waiter's sense of responsibility; it helped create a raving fan out of John Miller—and probably everyone in town who heard him tell the story.

LEADERSHIP CURRENCIES

Anyone who travels out of the country soon encounters the need to exchange currency for the currency of the present culture he or she is visiting. Just so, as organizations prepare to change, leaders must have a sense of the various leadership currencies available to help facilitate the process of re-visioning, reorganizing, and renewal.

Command is one type of leadership currency. This is the primary currency of authority and is embedded in the office or role of the leader. The domain where this is most effective—in fact, necessary—is the military. In that arena, orders are given and must be accepted—there is little room or time for persuasion or consensus. Command is effective—but it is not well-suited for most organizational cultures.

Charisma is a second type of leadership currency, which rests not in the office or authority of the leader but with his or her personality and ability to motivate and/or persuade. The charismatic leaders are those who seem to be *born* leaders and are often very effective. Yet one's presence and personality can go only so far. This is particularly true for the long-term leader. Over time, organizational members may become tone deaf after listening to the same voice for many years. What was so impressive and motivating at first may seem like the same old song over time. Charisma is a great gift—it is just not sufficient by itself for the long haul.

Consensus is another currency available to leaders. It is particularly effective when working with other capable leaders who want to be involved in the process of making the decision as well as implementing it. Consensus, however, takes time and can be a bit messy when working with large groups, strong personalities, and/or competing agendas. The end result, however, is generally worth the time and effort, for decisions and directions forged on this anvil have a certain staying power that can weather some setbacks and detours along the way.

Competence is fourth and an important type of currency. I sometimes illustrate this by asking, "Who would be the leader?" if a group from the university is taking a brief trip by school van or team bus and the vehicle breaks down. Picture the scene. The van limps off the highway to the safety of a rest area. Once it stops, everyone begins to file out. As we lift the hood and take turns looking at the engine, our "leadership" roles soon evaporate. The one who becomes the leader in such a moment is the one who can fix the van. Suddenly heads turn in his or her direction. That person's mechanical competency catapults that individual into a leadership role, at least until the group is back on the road.

As a university president I have the office and the authority that goes with the position. I also have good relationships with others and can work effectively with groups. But if I am to be effective over a long period of time, I must keep my administrative and educational competencies in shape. If for some reason I cannot track or engage in rigorous conversations about educational theory or university governance and culture, or if I cannot adjust to new ideas and technologies, the perception of my competence as a professional and leader may begin to wane. Leaders who last must continue to grow professionally and stay actively engaged in their fields of study. If not, they may be perceived as fine persons but not capable of skilled leadership.

Character is one more type of currency. This is often most visible when it is missing. The news is filled each day with powerful and capable people whose careers have been ruined by a character flaw. No one wants to follow a person who is not perceived as trustworthy.

Character is not a topcoat that can be taken up or laid aside depending upon the prevailing wind or the social climate. It is a person's *essential self* that flows from the values, faith, and commitments of the inner person. Emerson noted that "What lies behind us and what lies before us are tiny matters compared to what lies within us."

The significant thing about one's life is not what can be seen from the outside looking in; the significant thing is what is on the inside that flows ever so surely to the surface through one's actions and reactions. Greek philosopher Heraclitus summed it up in three words: *Character is destiny.*

Character is to be understood as the integrated set of a person's most fundamental attributes and tendencies. Moral perception, moral judgment, attitude formation, emotion, action, and reactions all blend to produce one's character. Having a good character involves integrity, honesty, patience, courage, kindness, generosity, and a strong sense of personal responsibility.

The world in which we live places great emphasis on the physical, intellectual, and social development of individuals. If only there were the same passion for character development. In the end, all education should seek to develop character. Without building a good character it is impossible to build a truly successful life.

ORGANIZATIONAL CULTURE

As the revision process continues, special attention must be given to both the nature of the administrative structure or structures and the normal procedures embedded in the history and practice of the organization. Often structures and procedures that were very effective at one time can become either ineffective or even counterproductive over time. Listening carefully to staff members as they describe what seems to be working well or what is particularly frustrating can begin to reveal those areas that need attention.

In addition to structural reorganization, which will be discussed later under the heading "Reticulation," leaders must also gage the nature of organizational culture. What often happens over time is that various subcultures develop to support the various functions of the organization. While this is natural and positive in many ways, it can nonetheless result in some levels of miscommunication, poor coordination, and an erosion of trust and confidence among the staff.

For example, the marketing and sales force of a company often develops a different mind-set from the accounting department or the student development staff or the admissions department and/or the traditional faculty and the overall academic culture of higher education. The people in accounting are, by design, process-and control-oriented. They function with a set of policies and procedures that are important for the financial management of the organization. On the other hand, the marketing team often wants and perhaps needs to color outside the lines, which can result in some organizational stress. Occasionally faculty members see their roles as teachers and researchers only, rather than as recruiters or student development officers.

Because various and sometimes competing functions are necessary within organizations, leaders must be able to foster an appreciation for these differences while maintaining enough compliance to protect the integrity of the organization and its control systems. It is important to stress the ways in which the various departments complement one another. At the university our admissions efforts are essential for the continued health and vitality of the school.

4

RE
SOLVE

Don't wait until everything is just right. It will never be perfect.
There will always be challenges, obstacles, and less-than-perfect conditions.
So what? Get started now. With each step you take, you will grow stronger
and stronger, more and more skilled, more and more self-confident,
and more and more successful.
—Mark Victor Hansen

What lies behind us and what lies before us are tiny matters
compared to what lies within us.
—Ralph Waldo Emerson

There are places in this world that are neither here nor there. Sometimes we experience moments along the way that are not quite now or then. And occasionally we have experiences that seem to be neither real nor imaginary.

These are the "in-between" places of life.

Sometimes these places are physical and fairly obvious. For some the shower is a place of suspended reality, where we think and drift and sing and imagine as well as bathe. An elevator is another example. It is a peculiar place that, in a way, is neither here nor there—where one is in between for a moment or two. It is a place where social norms are seemingly suspended and social interaction is often awkward. Does one speak or not speak, make eye contact or stare at the floor? I came across a list of fifteen things to do on an elevator to break the tension. For some reason my favorite on the list was number 14: "If there is just one other person on the elevator, reach around and tap him on the shoulder and then pretend it wasn't you."

Another such place is a jet-way, the corridor that telescopes out to an airplane. In the jet-way one is neither in the terminal nor on the plane. It is an "in-between" place.

At an international airport there is generally a passageway between where one disembarks and the arrivals' lounge, where a person goes to clear immigration and customs. Sometimes this is a long, circuitous passage. It is kind of a no-man's land: not in the country you left or on the plane, yet not quite in the country to which you are going. You are in-between.

I was in such a corridor years ago on a trip back from Africa. We were trudging along though a bland, blind passageway when we came suddenly to an escalator going down to the next level. The sight of those moving stairs froze an older African woman who was evidently traveling alone, perhaps for the first time.

She just stood there in wonder as she gazed at the stairs that were not really stairs.

The parade of passengers began backing up behind her, murmuring, mumbling, looking. A fellow traveler approached her gently and said, "Mama, let me walk with you," took her arm, and together they stepped onto the moving magic metal stairway. "I've never seen such a thing," I heard her say.

That woman moved in a single moment not just from one level of the terminal to another but from one culture to another, from one world to another.

We divide life into categories—time and space, mind and matter, spiritual and secular, present-past-future—and assume that we must be in one or the other of those various dimensions. But effective leaders are able to recognize other places and other moments in which one can experience and learn of things that cannot be discovered or apprehended in ordinary ways.

These are moments when we step back from the possible to be captured by the impossible, when we cease striving to achieve just long enough to reconnect with being, to be re-centered.

I am thinking of times and places and moments in life when we pause temporarily, as we do in those moments when, without really knowing it, we let our eyes come to a standstill in some space on the page of a book we've been reading in order to stare at something or at nothing at all.

It is as if we enter another world and stand in a third-person posture and gaze for a moment upon our life from out there. Have you had that experience where you are reading one moment and the next moment you are a million miles away with your eyes still fixed on the page? Are you still with me?

Often, however, it is those transitional moments that provide opportunity to revision and resolve to do things differently. These "in-between" times can be times of preparation—a jet-way, a doorway, an elevator from here to there. Such moments constitute a comma in the grammar of an organization's internal conversation about who they are, why they exist, and where they're headed. These are opportunities to go back to the future.

STARBUCKS: IT'S MORE THAN COFFEE

One of the books on my summer reading list a year or two ago was *Onward: How Starbucks Fought for Its Life Without Losing Its Soul.* The author is Howard Schultz, noted earlier, who was chairman, president, and chief executive officer of Starbucks Coffee.

For more than three decades Starbucks had a storied history of growth, soaring profits, and customer loyalty. But by 2008 the traits that made Starbucks successful were in jeopardy. Sales started to slide, the stock price plummeted, and the company's very survival seemed to be at risk.

To address the emerging problems, former CEO Howard Schultz, who had stepped aside almost eight years earlier to become chairman after growing Starbucks from eleven stores to more than eleven thousand stores, did something no one expected: he returned as CEO to oversee day-to-day operations. His goal was not just to stabilize the company but to transform it by refocusing on core values and reigniting the innovation and high level of customer service required to survive in a dramatically shifting marketplace. Schultz came back with passion and a plan. And in the course of two years— Starbucks returned to sustainable, profitable growth.[1]

I enjoyed the book, but it surprised me. I assumed the focus would be on leadership principles and business practices with a strong dose of either corporate or self-promotion mixed in. I was right, but I was wrong. Those things are embedded in the Starbucks story, but the focus and the power of the book rested in another domain.

Perhaps I should have known that—had I initially focused more intently on the subtitle of the book, *How Starbucks Fought for Its Life Without Losing Its Soul*. The primary emphasis of the book, and the thing that was so engaging to me, was the focus on the "soul" of Starbucks. In short, the thesis of the book is that in spite of its unparalleled success, Starbucks began to unintentionally shift its focus from its core values to its bottom line.

He goes on to suggest that an organization is at its heart the culmination of a set of intangibles. These do not seem to directly impact the revenue or profitability of a company, but they are the things that create and ultimately sustain the identity and texture of the business. Schultz cautions: "Forsaking them can take a subtle, collective toll."[2]

After returning to the company as CEO in 2008, Howard Shultz gathered his senior leadership team for a working retreat. They began their two days together by reviewing a single sheet of paper that had been in place for twenty-five years; it was the mission statement of Starbucks. Shultz writes,

> Starbuck's mission statement had never been just some framed piece of paper posted on our office walls. Perhaps more than any other company we had for years used our mission as a touchstone to make sure the guiding principles of how we run our business are intact and as a measuring stick for whether or not the company is aligned with its founding purpose. . . . Our mission provided guardrails for the company as we ventured down new roads, and every once in a while we looked in the rearview mirror to make sure we were being consistent. . . . It was from our mission that we had strayed.[3]

All organizations face such a temptation. In a 2011 speech to the faculty and staff of Olivet, I spoke of Howard Schultz's cautionary words and noted,

> In the recent past, Olivet has experienced strong growth and development as a university. We have been successful in almost any way you wish to measure it. Our academic programs have been significantly enriched, our faculty is stronger, and our staff is professional and proficient. Our undergraduate and graduate enrollments are at record levels. We are enlisting better students academically, and we are providing significantly more scholarships and grants than ever before to help worthy and needy students. Students in Free Enterprise excel in regional and national competitions, and projects from students in our honors program continue to be noteworthy.

Our chapel services and spiritual life emphases are strong, and our student development program is positive and energetic. Our intercollegiate athletic program is strong; we sent eleven teams to national tournaments last year, and we had thirteen teams recognized for their academic achievements.

All the while, we've been able to improve our campus and navigate our way through the toughest economic crisis since the Great Depression. And I think we have every right to look to the future with continued optimism and faith.

But the challenge for us as a university is to keep the center at the center, to grow without diminishing or straying from our mission, and to change without changing who we are.

There is no success for this university apart from living out our calling to provide "An Education with a Christian Purpose." It is this commitment to a Christian purpose that sets Olivet apart.

The overarching message and passion of Howard Schultz, as he returned to the daily operations of Starbucks, is that the company needed desperately to get back "to the core and make the changes necessary to evoke the heritage, the tradition, and the passion that we all have for the true Starbuck's Experience."[4]

Over time at the university as we began to look toward a new chapter of growth and development, I asked our faculty and staff to think about a series of questions.

What are the distinguishing characteristics of Olivet Nazarene University?

What are the things that set us apart from any other college or university?

What is it about Olivet that has the potential to change the lives of our students?

Why should we expect families to drive past a score of other colleges and universities to enroll their children here?

What is it that motivates men and women to provide strong financial support for the ongoing work of Olivet?

When a student graduates from Olivet, what marks of the university should the student take with him or her?

All of these get folded ultimately into a single overarching question: *What is it that makes Olivet, Olivet?* I was convinced that we needed to be able to corporately respond to that final question. Surely there would be some differences of opinion and perspective, but nonetheless I wanted to engender a significant level of shared convictions about the nature of our collective work.

In the book *Above All Else* I tell the story of an office building on the outskirts of London that began to develop a series of severe structural cracks. These cracks first appeared on the upper floors of the building. No one seemed too alarmed in the beginning. The cracks were considered the result of some natural settling which occasionally occurs a few years after a building is completed. But the cracks grew greater and began to spread from floor to floor.

Builders and engineers were summoned to the site, but no one at first could determine the source of the problem. Everything appeared to be in order. Finally the building architect, who had retired by then, was brought back to the site for consultation. After a careful inspection, he asked to be taken to the basement of the building. He then proceeded down through a series of sub-basements that housed some of the mechanical systems.

When he reached the lowest level, he discovered the cause of the problem. One large supporting wall in that sub-basement had mysteriously been removed. He reported that the cause of the problem had nothing to do with the fourteenth floor, where the cracks had first appeared—the problem was with the foundation.

An investigation was launched, and it was soon determined that a worker whose job was housed in that lower basement had begun years before taking a brick or two out of one of many load-bearing walls as he left work each day. Over time he accumulated enough bricks to build a small garage at his house. At first it appeared that no one would know, for rarely did other people come to the sub-basement. What he didn't realize was that, sooner or later, the results of a weakened foundation always eventually appear in some part of the building.

All the patching, painting, and propping-up in the world will not make up for a faulty foundation.[5] That is true architecturally, but it is also true with organizations. There are times when leaders must go deep to inspect and repair the foundations of their organizations. This is particularly true for those who lead in the same place over a long period of time.

THE BIGGEST LOSER

The long-running success of the television show *The Biggest Loser* is an interesting phenomenon. It is a reality show that follows overweight contestants who are attempting to lose weight. They compete against other contestants to win a cash prize and achieve the personal goal of improved fitness, appearance, and health. The show began in 2004 and has sustained strong ratings ever since.

In addition to the hype and drama, the promise of money, and a measure of fame, these contestants at the heart of the show are in fact competing not against others but against themselves, their past failures, and uncertain futures. The real power of the show rests with the personal stories of the contestants that unfold week after week amidst a mixture of laughter and tears, success and setbacks.

The show dramatizes just how hard it is to sustain change and progress over time. Contestants demonstrate what almost anyone who has tried to lose weight or conquer an addiction or break a bad habit knows: to succeed in almost any endeavor takes more effort than expected, takes longer than one wishes, is a process filled with interruptions and setbacks, and once attained is hard to maintain.

This is true for weight loss and fitness, but it is also true for those who seek to build or rebuild a business or organization: it is a harder, longer, more frustrating process than first imagined. There really aren't any quick fixes or easy answers; leadership takes commitment, discipline, and time. "While we dream there are easy paths or hope we will find a genie to make our wishes come true, the reality is that hard work, action, and perseverance are the only "fairy dust" that will fulfill our dreams."[6]

Nonetheless, re-visioning an organization can be done, and when it begins to happen, good things follow, and the process gets easier as one rides the crest of momentum and positive energy.

THE CIRCUS CAME TO TOWN

The circus comes to Chicago, the closest large city to where I live, for a week or two each year. During its last visit, I was reading a news story about it in which a reporter was relating a conversation he had with one of the guys who does the high-wire tight-rope walking far above the audience. This particular acrobat was one of those fellows who worked without a net.

"What does it take," the reporter asked the tightrope walker, "to do what you do?"

"Three things," he answered. "Courage. Balance. But most of all, concentration; you fix your eyes on that wire, and until it's all over you never shift your attention."

"Never," he added firmly.

Where one sets his or her gaze is very important, isn't it? What we see—what we give attention to—shapes our thinking, our experience, and in some cases our destiny. Controlling our focus is particularly important for leaders. "Fix your eyes on that wire," the tightrope walker said.

If one looks at the wrong things or sets his or her gaze in the wrong direction, if he or she glances off the mark or concentrates on things that distract—it is very easy to stumble. The content of your vision determines much of the course and character of your life.

Leadership is a high-wire act, no doubt about it. That is particularly true for an organization that needs renewal—for that means change. Yet confident and strong leaders can effectively enlist and enable the various stakeholders to come together to fashion a preferred future for the organization. The leader can and will make the difference. As Napoleon once declared, "An army of rabbits commanded by a lion is better than an army of lions commanded by a rabbit."[7]

KILIMANJARO

A few years ago when I made the climb to the summit of Mt. Kilimanjaro, there were many times I had to keep telling myself, *Having fun is not always fun.* I had to narrow my focus at certain points on the journey, simply taking the next step and then the next and then the next. Little by little, over time, the mountain became manageable. It was not easy, and it was often not much fun. However, the view from top was spectacular. Only those who keep going ever get to see it.

While I admire and try to encourage folks to think out of the box, I also realize that most of our work is done *in* the box. We may wish things were different—that we had better resources, fewer issues, and different ways of working—yet the truth is that we work where we work, with whom we work, doing the work that needs to be done, and therefore we can't always step outside the box. We have to renew ourselves and infuse meaning and value into the daily work we are called to do. Most of us cannot afford the luxury of blaming our lack of success on issues other than our own performance. As the saying goes, "A poor sailor blames the wind."

I am often encouraged by the promise contained in the writings of the Hebrew prophet Jeremiah in which he says, "'I know the plans I have for you,' declares the LORD, 'plans to prosper you and not to harm you, plans to give you hope and a future.'"

SECTION 2
THE LOOK WITHIN

5
RE
ENGAGE

Do not wait until the conditions are perfect to begin.
Beginning makes the conditions perfect.
—Alan Cohen

As one begins the next phase of re-visioning, it is vital that a process of reengagement takes place. Leadership, like life itself, is a journey that involves a daily discipline and an ongoing engagement. A leader must ensure that he or she remains fully engaged in the life of the organization over the long haul. That does not happen automatically. Leadership is wearing and can, over time, diminish one's continued enthusiasm. David McNally includes the following oft-repeated story in his book *Even Eagles Need a Push:*

Jimmy's mother called out to him at seven in the morning, "Jimmy, get up. It's time for school." There was no answer. She called again, this time more loudly, "Jimmy, get up! It's time for school!" Once more there was no answer. Exasperated, she went to his room and shook him, saying, "Jimmy, it is time to get ready for school!"

He answered, "Mother, I'm not going to school. There are fifteen hundred kids at that school, and every one of them hates me. I'm not going to go."

"Get to school," she replied sharply.

"But Mother, all the teachers hate me, too. I saw three of them talking the other day, and one of them was pointing his finger at me. I know they all hate me, so I'm not going to school," Jimmy answered.

"Get to school!" his mother demanded again.

"But Mother, I don't understand it. Why would you want to put me through all of that torture and suffering?" he protested.

"Jimmy, for two good reasons," she fired back. "First, you're forty-two years old. Second, you're the principal."[1]

Perhaps every leader has had a few mornings like that. What one cannot afford to do is hide beneath the covers. Detachment is a danger for the long-term leader. Over time there comes the subtle temptation to withdraw and reduce one's active engagement to only those aspects of the work that are most rewarding.

In my world as a university president, this shows up in the following ways. After ten, fifteen, or twenty years of attending student council retreats, staff meetings, faculty gatherings, recitals, art shows, plays, concerts, alumni gatherings, ballgames, dinners, community events, and so on, one is soon tempted to listen to the small inner voice that asks, *Do I really have to go to another event tonight? Will it matter if I miss?*

What happens when one misses a single event is that nothing happens. There is no outcry that the president wasn't there—people understand that the leader can't possibly attend everything. This non-response from others makes it easier the next week to skip another event and so on. To occasionally withdraw from the din of leadership is not a fatal flaw; in fact, it is necessary if one is to pace himself or herself for the long run. But the problem comes when little by little the occasional "absence" becomes a pattern of non-engagement.

Some years ago I got to know an individual who had served as college president at a couple of schools for a total of more than twenty years. By the end of his last term of service he was detached from his board, suspicious of faculty, and annoyed by students. I remember thinking, *This fellow is in the wrong line of work.* Faculty and students are the heart of a university—those are the people who make things happen, and it is with them that the mission of the school is most fully realized. Therefore, if one is to maintain influence, leaders must stay *actively* engaged. An effective leader is one who is not satisfied to leave well enough alone.

CONVERSATIONS WITH THE PRESIDENT

At the ten-year mark of my leadership at the university, I sensed a need to reengage with the faculty and staff. All the "new" of my leadership had worn off; the honeymoon had ended. We had adjusted to life together, and there was the possibility that things were becoming a bit routine. Like the married couple who sits quietly at the breakfast table not having anything new to say, I felt compelled to strike up a new round of conversations.

To help facilitate this reengagement, I hosted a round of informal "Conversations with the President." Over the course of the next academic year, I arranged for a large number of lunches, morning coffees, and afternoon Coke breaks, then circulated the schedule to faculty and staff, who were invited to sign up for a time that fit their schedules. Attendance was limited to twelve at a time. We met in the President's Dining Room for an hour or so.

At each gathering I was pleased to see a random mix of individuals from various departments across the spectrum of the university. This was an important part of the dynamic, for it fostered a broader array of viewpoints and freed the participants from set patterns that would be in place if we had met by departments. Senior leadership—the vice presidents—were asked not to participate; I wanted it to be a moment when it was just the president listening and participating in a conversation.

During the planning phase for this listening initiative, I discussed the idea with a college president friend. He paid close attention, affirmed my plans, then added one word of caution. "Since you're calling these gatherings 'Conversations with the President,' there had better be conversation. If you do all the talking, the whole endeavor could result in having the very opposite impact for which you are hoping." He then recalled a group dynamic principle that says, "Remember—no one really owns a meeting until he or she has spoken."

Armed with his advice and eager to strengthen my relationships with faculty and staff, I began the process, which proved to be more productive and helpful than I imagined. At the beginning of each gathering I asked each person to introduce himself or herself and tell the group something about himself or herself that might be unexpected. This immediately energized the group by drawing each participant into the beginning moments of the conversation.

I followed with a single, open-ended question that represented the core for the conversation. I asked, "What is it like to work at Olivet Nazarene University?" At first the groups were tentative, perhaps not know exactly what I was looking for—but soon, as one or two ventured forth with an answer, others picked up a thread from the conversation and elaborated, questioned, or perhaps even contradicted a given perception. Little by little, each discussion took on a life of its own.

As the conversations continued I would ask, "If you could change one thing to make Olivet a better place, what would that be?" As different ones in the group spoke, I made notes of questions that I would need to follow up on and recorded the essence of suggestions and concerns. My primary goals for these conversations were to listen, and by listening to affirm each individual and to inspire an added measure of institutional buy-in on the part of each participant.

I prepared an executive summary of the overarching comments and concerns that surfaced in those conversations and shared that information with the administrative team. In the many months following those discussions I was pleased to sense a deepened personal connection with the individuals with whom I had shared a meal or a cup of coffee.

In later encounters with faculty, staff, students, and several off-campus constituent groups, I often asked individuals to complete the statement "Olivet is at its best when . . ." The responses served two purposes. First, those who were asked the question were prompted to think about the university at its best. Second, the various answers provided me with important feedback.

To formalize this kind of feedback we decided to annually participate in a national survey of "best Christian workplaces."[2] This survey is administered anonymously and scored confidentially by a separate third-party organization. Doing this has provided an annual assessment and longitudinal look at workplace issues. It has also provided a basis for some objective discussions across campus about the nature of our working environment and the ways we relate to each other.

Those types of discussions are a vital component in creating a culture of nonjudgmental evaluation and ongoing renewal. Marshall McLuhan suggested that on "spaceship earth" there are no passengers, only crew. His point was that everyone has a responsibility for the welfare of the planet. Just so, the renewal of a business or organization is fueled in part by the conviction that ours is a joint success. Recently I chose as the theme for our annual

President's Dinner for Faculty and Staff the phrase "What we do here we do together." This theme, and my opening address for that year, reinforced the interrelated nature of our life and work.

When I was first elected president of the university, a veteran college administrator wrote me a note of congratulations and included the following words of advice: "To succeed as a college president, start out running as fast as you can, and then, over time, pick up the pace!" It hasn't quite been like that, but almost. It is a demanding and high-visibility profession. Leading a university is more than a full-time position—it is a way of life, and little by little one learns how to pace the work for sustainability over the long hall.

STANDING IN A CIRCLE

In the early years of my work I came to realize that I was metaphorically standing in the middle of a circle surrounded by various stakeholders and constituents who had their own perspectives and priorities. At one place on the circle stood the students— thousands of them—each viewing the university and me and my leadership through the single lens of their individual experiences.

As I turned to give the students my attention, I became aware that at another point on the circle stood parents whose expectations and demands for the university were not always the same as those of the students. And there were faculty members standing in the circle and staff members, community leaders, board members, alumni, donors, accrediting groups, government agencies, and so on. I was the only one in the middle, and all those various constituents had a legitimate voice as to the functioning of the school. I knew intuitively that the groups would not all finally speak with one voice.

I came to realize that my role and responsibility as president was not to coerce or cajole all the groups to move to the same place on the circle; that simply was not going to happen. My task as the leader was to ask and inspire those individuals to join hands, thus affirming each other's perspective and linking their interests to an overarching vision of what Olivet should and can be.

Howard Schultz writes, "I've never bought into the notion that there is a single recipe for successful leadership. But I do think effective leaders share two intertwined attributes: an unbridled level of confidence about where their organizations are headed, and the ability to bring people along."[3] It is this act of actively enlisting people to embrace a vision of the future that lies at the heart of the engagement strategy. Wayne Lambert, Vice President of Strategic Alliances for Schneider Electric, notes, "Success happens only when people are fully engaged and respected by those in leadership. There is no winning alone."[4]

Years ago when I was a boy and the New York Yankees had won yet another World Series, which they seemed to do every year during that era, a reporter was interviewing a player named Lefty Gomez, a star pitcher for the Yankees, and asked this question: "Lefty, what is the secret of your success?"

"Clean livin' and a fast outfield," he replied.

What he was saying was this: Even when I give it my very best effort—when I throw my finest pitch—even then, on occasion, someone will hit the ball over my head and beyond my reach. When that happens, my success, my win/loss record, is in the hands of my teammates. Someone else has to catch the ball, make the throw, or get the hit.

Lefty understood the idea of team. He was a star, but his success was embedded in their success. It is true with us as well. We are in this together.

Some years ago as I was walking across a crowded public square, I spotted a young man coming toward me wearing a T-shirt with a slogan written on it in simple but bold letters: "Be yourself, only better." What a great thought for individuals and for institutions! Each business or organization must find—then embrace—its own identity and strive daily to be its best self.

Each leader must also be his or her best self. One avenue for leadership and thus organizational renewal is the development of a certain agility—the ability to respond easily and react without losing one's balance, focus, or forward momentum.

LEADERSHIP AGILITY AS A PART OF RE-ENGAGEMENT

Bill Joiner and Stephen Josephs have published a major work that explores the concept of leadership agility in-depth. Their book is called *Leadership Agility: Five Levels of Mastery for Anticipating and Initiating Change.*[5] The book opens with a brief case study of an individual named Robert who becomes president of a struggling Canadian oil company. The company was in the early stages of decline; earnings were dropping, morale was at an all-time low, and people were frustrated and unhappy.

The new CEO quickly realized that he must actively engage the entire company in birthing a renewed vision, which would give rise to new structures and systems that would allow the company to proactively respond to the changing economic environment. "If fact, his vision was to develop an organization whose business performance and innovative ways of operating would be benchmarked by companies from a wide variety of industries. Robert overturned his predecessor's assumption that the company's options were limited to difficult but familiar cost-cutting solutions. Instead, he decided to create a set of break-out strategies that would develop a more innovative organization."[6]

Joiner and Josephs write, "Leadership agility is directly analogous to organizational agility: It's the ability to take wise and affective action amid complex, rapidly changing conditions."[7] They identify five levels of leadership agility: the Expert Level, the Achiever Level, the Catalyst Level, the Co-Creator Level, and the Synergist Level. Not every leader can or should seek to function in all levels; however, if one is to sustain effective and fresh leadership with the same organization over a long period of time, he or she should move to at least some measure of expression at each level.

The **Expert Level** of agility is expressed in a leader's ability to solve problems. The focus at this level of leadership is to develop subject-matter expertise based on the assumption that one's leadership ability rests on his or her expertise and positional authority. This, however, is a flawed concept, because experts are the least agile managers. Expertise is important, but it can also focus so much of one's attention on problem-solving at a micro-level that a leader fails to think about global change for the organization. Therefore, the leader who is seeking to reengage an organization's drive and creativity must do more than try to perfect the systems already in place. This might result in some incremental improvement but would fall short of actively inspiring a new chapter of organizational development.

The **Achiever Level** is that in which the leader and his or her organization can accomplish their desired outcomes. The focus shifts from expertise and process to outcomes. What have we achieved? That is the overarching question.

The **Catalyst Level** refers to leaders who can mobilize break-out endeavors. They are open to change and are willing to rethink existing assumptions. This generally results in the development of a participative culture where the whole is substantially greater than the sum of the parts. The catalytic leader builds on an appropriate level of expertise and focuses on achievements empowered by vision and participation. "Catalysts, with their openness to change, their willingness to rethink basis assumptions, and their visionary orientation, represent the first level of agility capable of sustained success in today's highly complex, constantly changing business environment."[8]

At the **Co-Creator Level** leaders have a keen sense of how everything in their organizations is interdependent. Thus, there is a strong, steady commitment to the common good and fostering collaboration and teambuilding. These leaders work to develop collaborative and organizational relationships that are rooted in a deep sense of shared purpose and mission. At this level, energy and creativity become shared in a new way that reengages individuals throughout the organization to think and act in new ways while staying in close touch with others.

The **Synergist Level** describes leaders who evoke unexpected possibilities. This is a much more subtle distinction. One of the differences at this level is that leaders begin to engage in a more fluid, moment-to-moment flow. "As this capacity for present-centered awareness develops, it gives leaders the ability, in contentious and chaotic situations, to stand in the eye of the storm."[9]

These distinctions are not to be confused as leadership styles or personality types. They are better understood as sequential stages of leadership development. Leaders first solve problems, meet their goals, and then foster a new culture of openness to change and innovation that leads to increased interdependence and the enabling of unexpected results.

Joiner and Josephs write, "As organizational theorists have pointed out, to enjoy sustained success, companies need to develop a level of organizational agility that matches the increasing level of change and complexity in their business environment."[10]

BE VISIBLE AND REINTRODUCE YOURSELF

I have found it helpful to occasionally reintroduce myself to those I lead and to those with whom I work most closely. It is easy and perhaps only natural that, over time, our interest in and appreciation of others dims a bit. For example, in my world I sometimes think, *These folks have heard all I have to say, so how can I cast a new vision or motivate the team again and again and again?*

To counter this natural trend, effective leaders learn to reinvent themselves, not in a shallow or duplicitous way by trying to become something they are not, but by continually growing and developing both personally and professionally. I know that from time to time I need to freshen my leadership language with new insights and examples, so that even over a long period of time people will feel that I have something new to say.

I am generally a suit-and-tie guy who lives next to the campus yet still drives to work. My leadership style, personality, experience, and professional approaches are highly traditional. This is reflected in my interaction and public life with others; what you see is what you get. I think that generally this wears well over time. There is something good about solid predictability that suggests one can be counted on as a reliable leader.

But every now and then across the years, I have been able to find a way to show another side of my personality that serves to reengage and freshen my relationships on campus. Four quick examples come to mind. The first, and most dramatic, was my decision a few years ago to climb Mt. Kilimanjaro, the highest peak in Africa and the tallest free-standing volcano in the world.

Flying to Tanzania and joining a small group of strangers in the attempt to climb one of the world's great mountains was more than just out of the box—it was out of this world, or at least out of *my* world. The trip became a conversation point on campus, and when I returned I was able to speak to a variety of campus and community groups about my experience. The photographs of me in climbing clothes and a backpack after nine days on the mountain, having not shaved or showered, provided a dramatic contrast to the buttoned-up president who is seen every day walking the campus.

But there was more; the Kilimanjaro experience began to inform my conversations and speeches, not in a laborious or boring manner—that is, "Will he ever stop talking about the climb?"—but in a measured and reflective way. I was able to suggest that life is filled with mountains: raising a family, leading a team at work, completing a graduate degree, dealing with an unexpected illness, and so on. And there were certain principles I learned on the climb that applied to much of life.[11]

Another "new me" showed up on campus when I agreed to take a part in a major spring musical on campus. The drama director sent me an e-mail saying, "Dr. Bowling, I am in the process of casting for the music to be presented next semester. There is a part for an older, grouchy neighbor—would you have an interest in joining the cast? I think it could draw attention and, in turn, give a boost to the theater program."

A "grouchy old neighbor" who sings? Me? I agreed and began the process of learning my lines and the songs. I also started to grow a mustache and goatee for the part. The theater was packed for every performance. Faculty, staff, students, and community folks took great interest in this generally hidden side of the university president.

On another occasion, while attending a student fall festival in the middle of the campus quad, I stood with our Vice President for Student Development, watching students ride, or at least trying to ride, a mechanical bull that had been placed in a makeshift coral of straw. After two or three students had hit the dust, someone called out, "Dr. Bowling, you're next!" I waved as if to say thanks but no thanks. But in response, a chant began to move through the crowd: "Dr. B.—Dr. B.—Dr. B."

Against my better judgment, I agreed. A cheer rose, and students from other parts of the quad began to crowd in. I handed my wallet and cell phone to my colleague and walked into the ring. I could tell from watching the other riders that there were variable speeds available and that those speeds and the direction of the bull could be controlled by the operator, who stood to the side holding a small black control box. During the cheering, as I was getting ready to mount, I walked past the operator at the controls and said, "Seth, you gotta help me here."

"I got your back, Dr. B." he replied.

The crowd quieted as I stood for a moment at the side of the bull. I said, "Everybody ready?"

"Ready!" came the reply.

Then, without any further hesitation, I grabbed the saddle horn and swung myself up onto the bull.

"Any last words?" someone called out.

"For Alma Mater, Olivet," I replied. "Hit it!"

Just then Seth, the young man with the black box, hit the switch—and the bull came alive. I don't remember much after that, just lots of twisting, turning, and tossing about with me hanging on for dear life.

After about a minute—which seemed like an hour—I leaned one way, just as the bull bucked and turned sharply in the other direction. That was all it took. Suddenly I was sailing through the air. I landed hard with my right arm under me. A couple of students helped me up, and I waved like a champion to the crowd, but there was a strong, sharp pain in my side, and I could hardly take a deep breath. The following day it was determined that I had cracked a rib. But it was worth it. I had a whole new set of conversations with students—as well as faculty and staff members—who had heard of my ride.

About fifteen years into my tenure as president, the university reestablished its marching band program. The goal was to create the largest marching band among the more than one hundred colleges and universities of the Council for Christian Colleges and Universities, which is our primary peer group. Students were recruited, music scholarships were increased, a new director was hired, new uniforms were ordered, and a large banner appeared on one of the campus buildings declaring, "Strike Up the Band!" The campus began to catch band fever.

The band's first public performance was scheduled for the first home football game. Two weeks before the big night, I contacted the band director and told him that I would like to march—*incognito*—with the band for their debut performance. He loved the idea. He delivered a band uniform to my house and told me where to be and what to expect.

When the big day came, I donned the uniform, plumed hat an all, dusted off my trombone, which I had not played in many years, and made my way to the band staging area, where the few students who knew of my plan met me and took me to my designated position. The plan was simple: I was to follow the student in front of me and stay in step with the students on either side. I could hold my trombone to my mouth, but they ask me *not* to play. "Just pretend," one of the students said.

He must have heard me practicing, I thought.

Soon we were off, marching toward the football stadium, then onto the field for the pregame opening. As the band took the field, the crowd cheered. After reaching our designated places, the band turned toward the home stand and played a rousing fanfare.

The public address announcer welcomed the band and then asked, "Is Dr. Bowling in the stands? Surely he is here tonight! Has anyone seen our university president?"

As the crowd looked around the stands, the lead trumpet player in the band played a loud series of notes to direct everyone's attention back to the field.

The public address announcer then said, "Ladies and gentlemen, I see the president. He is on the field, marching with the band." At that point, my trombone section played a few notes, and I stepped forward, took off my hat and bowed to the crowd. It was great fun!

The musical, the mountain climbing, the mechanical bull, and the marching band provided a series of moments of reengagement. Those things alone would have had little impact if I had not also been conducting the "Conversations with the President" and doing the more serious work of reengagement; but coupled with the more important efforts, these events seemed to freshen my ongoing engagement with the campus community.

Leaders who serve over long periods of time increase their effectiveness by reengaging and freshening the relationships and meaningful conversations they have with others in the organization. A synergy develops that can result in new ideas and a cultural shift that recaptures the energy and passion to excel. There is an African proverb that says, "If you wish to travel fast, go alone. If you wish to travel far, go together." The leader who can continually reengage the organization in meaningful ways will go far.

6

RE
PAIR

Failure is the opportunity to begin again more intelligently.
—Henry Ford

---

*There are some things one can achieve only by
a deliberate leap in the opposite direction.*
—Franz Kafka

Have you ever seen a boat in dry dock? It is the place where boats
are lifted from the water for the purpose of cleaning and repairing
the hull. Not only is water generally corrosive, but sea water is
particularly so, which means that boats need a regular cleaning. It
is important to remove the buildup of various forms of debris for
the long-term condition of the boat. In left untended, this debris
builds up and has the effect of slowing a boat down because of the
added resistance in the water. A well-maintained boat minimizes
this drag and allows for maximum efficiency. But more important, the corrosive nature of the buildup will impair the integrity
and long-term viability of the boat's hull. The dry-docking process also allows for a careful inspection to detect potential problems before they occur.

Although the public demonstration of one's leadership takes place primarily out in the open sea where the vitality of an organization is put to the test, both leaders and their organizations ought to have occasional periods in dry dock. Regardless of one's age, individuals naturally accumulate a set of experiences over time that in turn color a person's perceptions and create certain assumptions, which may have been true at one time but no longer present a clear picture of reality.

An effective leader schedules times to push the pause button and mute the sound long enough to evaluate the health of his or her organization. This can be done through annual reviews, planning and evaluative retreats, along with various forms of performance audits and professional consultations.

Years ago I got to know a very successful business owner whose financial and overall business acumen was legendary. His manufacturing business was in a rural area of the Midwest, which partly explained his modest lifestyle. He lived in a modest house and never displayed the accoutrements of wealth. His one exception was that he decided to purchase an imported luxury automobile from a dealer in the state capital many miles away.

Over time, as is the normal routine for such cars, it needed some specialized service. In response, he would have to make the trip into the city where he had purchased the vehicle and wait while it was being serviced and then drive home. That practice soon became an irritant, so he decided to make just one trip a year to the dealership. In the interim, he had the curious practice of placing a piece of masking tape over the various warning lights as they came on, ignoring not just the normal warnings but also the potentially serious signals as well. After a couple of years of this, he returned to driving a car that could be serviced in his own community. Just as one routinely schedules a car for maintenance, so must a leader provide for regular tune-ups.

- Take time to work—it is the price of success.
- Take time to think—it is the source of power.
- Take time to play—it is the secret of perpetual youth.
- Take time to read—it is the fountain of wisdom.
- Take time to be friendly—it is the road to happiness.
- Take time to love and be loved—it is nourishment for the soul.
- Take time to share—it is too short a life to be selfish.
- Take time to laugh—it is the magic of the heart.
- Take time to dream—it is hitching your wagon to a star.[1]

FINGERPRINTS AND TOUCHSTONES

Forensic scientists tell us that no two human fingerprints are the same. Even identical twins have different fingerprints. Therefore, individuals can be identified solely by their prints; a person's presence at a certain place can be verified by the fingerprints left behind. What this means is that every human hand looks essentially the same, yet every one is distinctly different.

In the same way it may seem to some that all colleges and universities are essentially the same; some larger, some publicly funded, some research based, but they all have a campus, a set of courses, a group of individuals to reach, and so on. If that is true, the task of choosing a college or university would become relatively easy; one could choose the least expensive or the closest school or some other rather generic criteria, since all schools are alike.

However, just like human hands, colleges, universities, and all other businesses and organizations have their own set of fingerprints. Business may be similar, yet each still has a culture and ethos that uniquely express that particular institution. I sometimes tell prospective students and their families that if we could dust the world for fingerprints, we would find the prints of Olivet showing up in thousands of places: businesses, schools, hospitals, computer labs, counseling offices, research facilities, and scores of other venues.

Do you know what a *touchstone* is—where that word came from? A touchstone is a hard black stone, such as jasper or basalt, that was used in days gone by to test the quality of gold or silver by comparing the streak left on the stone by one of these metals with that of a standard alloy.

Use of the touchstone revolutionized the concept of money. Prior to its introduction, gold and silver were common currencies, but these could easily be mixed with less expensive metals—tin and lead were common—that made them less expensive to produce. But once those lesser metals were introduced, it was difficult to distinguish pure gold from "fools' gold," so to speak.

The touchstone made it possible to test for such forgeries quickly and efficiently and also to determine the relative value of different alloys. That paved the way for gold and silver to become the standard equivalents of value and eventually to a system of government-issued standard currency guaranteed by the mint. This virtually eliminated the forgeries.

Preserving, fostering, and celebrating the individual characteristics of a given business is one important task of leadership. If leaders and/or organizations lose touch with the touchstone, what follows will be a loss of core identity.

A FENCE OR A POLE

Thinking about a shared identity can be considered from two contrasting points of view. One could talk about a fence or a pole.

A fence sets definite boundaries—you can go this far but no farther. If you are going to be part of this organization or this group, you must stay within the fence. This approach can become more of a complicating factor rather than a simplifying one in some cases, because individuals may not always agree on where the fence should be. In addition, a fence mentality sets limits on one's thinking and may restrict helpful input from other individuals or organizations that do things differently. Just as a fence may keep us in—it might also keep others out.

Fences are not bad; they often serve a good purpose. But perhaps there is a better way to think about an organization's shared identity. Organizations are not formed as an association of fence-builders; that is not what gives birth to new companies or new programs and projects within an existing organization. The early focus is not on a fence but on a pole.

What does that mean? The pole is that thing in the middle around which an organization rallies. It is what draws people together. A fence coerces people to stay within the boundary. A clear, strongly articulately and widely embraced vision or plan can unify a varied group of people for a common cause. In fact, if the pull of the pole is strong enough, one would never be in danger of climbing the fence. Leaders who successfully re-vision organizations are able to repair the pole—that unifying center around which people gather.

A centering and unifying force for the renewal of Starbucks was Howard Schultz's transformation agenda, which was articulated in early 2008. This consisted of what he called Seven Pillars:

- Be the undisputed coffee authority
- Engage and inspire our partners
- Ignite the emotional attachment with our customers
- Expand our global presence
- Be a leader in ethical sourcing and environmental impact
- Create innovative growth platforms worthy of our coffee
- Deliver a sustainable economic model.[2]

REBUILDING THE WALL

There is a great story in the Bible about a period of repair in the life of the Jewish people. They had been conquered by the invading army of Babylon. The walls of the city had been destroyed. The palaces, the Temple, and the homes of the city were ransacked, and a large number of people were taken into captivity. The city of Jerusalem lay in ruin for decades. Finally a leader named Nehemiah, one of those who had been taken into captivity, was permitted to return to Jerusalem to rebuild the wall. It's a great story of how with a fresh vision, clear leadership, and steady work, a city—and with it a people—was rebuilt.

Renewing one's organization and personal leadership follows the same formula: vision, leadership, and careful work. Often the place to begin to foster genuine and lasting renewal is to repair strained or broken relationships. It would not be unusual for an individual in senior leadership over many years in the same location to accumulate some interpersonal baggage. If those points of natural stress and strain are not cared for, they eventually can undermine a leader's effectiveness.

Renewing relationships begins within. Marshall Goldsmith identifies twenty habits that hold people back and prevent leaders from succeeding. Many of these behaviors become critical as one ascends the leadership ladder and/or when a leader is in place over a long period of time and those behaviors become habits. He writes,

> Jack Welch has a Ph.D. in chemical engineering, but I doubt if any problems he encountered in his last thirty years at General Electric were in any way related to his skill at chemical titration or formulating plastics. When he was vying for the CEO job, the issues holding him back were strictly behavioral—his brashness, his blunt language, his unwillingness to suffer fools.[3]

Goldsmith's list of twenty habits is this:

1. Winning too much: This manifests itself in the need, perhaps the obsession to always win. There is a fine distinction between wanting to win and having to win. When one is fanatical about winning, it can result in a host of poor interpersonal behaviors and faulty judgments. Goldsmith says, "Winning too much is easily the most common behavioral problem that I observe in successful people."[4]

2. Adding too much value: This is the tendency to overvalue your opinion or perspective. It shows up in comments such as "Well, I suppose that would work, but I think it should be this way." If this type of response is given too often, without much serious consideration, it can undercut the creativity of others and/or their willingness to suggest new ideas. Perhaps a leader's idea might work, but if those ideas always trump the suggestions of others, such actions can reduce the other person's ownership and enthusiasm for the project or task at hand.

I had a very fine colleague I supervised in one of the organizations where I served. When I left that job to accept another position, the individual who followed me was very capable but perhaps a bit overconfident. He constantly pointed out to this colleague of mine who was still working there that no matter what was done or suggested, it could be just a little better. The constant correction and expression of dissatisfaction with how things were done broke the spirit of my former colleague. He ended up soon finding another job. His joy was gone.

3. Passing judgment: This is an amplification of the need to express one's opinion on everything, which takes the form of rating others and evaluating their ideas with a bias that rests on the conviction that your opinion is superior simply because you are the leader.

About five years into my work at Olivet, one of our new senior managers came to me with an idea that would dramatically change how things were done in his area. I knew instinctively that he was wrong and probably would have said so had he not been new. I didn't want his first big idea to be shot down immediately, so I thought, *Hold steady and let him learn for himself that this won't work here. Then use that failure as a teaching moment to evaluate with him what should have been done.* So in response to his request to make a set of changes, I said, "Well, I'm not sure how that will work, but give it a try." Off he went, eager to leave his own personal stamp on the work of his department.

Much to my surprise, his initiatives worked wonderfully well and brought an air of fresh enthusiasm to everything that happened in his area. It continues to bear fruit today. When I realized that he was right and I was wrong, I remember telling myself to learn from this—that not every idea has to be my idea! I discovered a refreshing freedom in that simple—now obvious—observation. In the early years of my tenure, I felt it was all up to me; after all, I was in charge. I now understand and often celebrate the fact that it is *not* all up to me. What a relief!

4. Making destructive comments: Too often individuals fall into a subconscious pattern of making comments that end up building walls rather than bridges between those with whom we work. This is essentially a psychological defense mechanism to reinforce the administrative pecking order. When a leader quickly and sometimes smugly dismisses a suggestion or comment from another member of the team, it may serve to reinforce in the leader's mind the fact that he or she is the boss; but it simultaneously prompts the one who made the comment to think, *I won't do that again,* or *He [She] never cares about anyone's ideas but his [her] own.*

This not only shuts down communication and creativity but also devalues the people involved, creates distance, and often produces negative feelings. Goldsmith suggests, "For one week treat every idea that comes your way from another person with complete neutrality. Think of yourself as a human Switzerland. Don't take sides."[5] Obviously, not every idea is a good one, and there is a need in any organization for candor, but the wise leader uses discretion in how he or she initially responds to the input from others. The leader may believe that he or she is simply judging an idea; however, the employee may feel that he or she is being judged personally and often publicly.

5. Use of wrong language. The tendency to pass judgment and make a negative comment can take the subtle form of starting one's response to another with "On the other hand," "But," or "However." These qualifiers may be correct, but that may not be the place to start as one processes the ideas and comments of others. This language suggests that the one using the qualifiers is right, regardless of the other person's input. Regardless of how well-intentioned those comments might be, they carry the tone of "You are wrong, and let me tell you why." No one likes to be on the receiving end of that kind of message.

6. Telling the world how smart you are: This is another variation of this need to win. "*Being* smart turns people on. *Announcing* how smart you are turns them off."[6]

7. Speaking when angry: When you think of legendary college basketball coach Bobby Knight, what is the first thing you think of—his more than eight hundred victories or his three NCAA titles? Probably not. Those accomplishments are significant and noteworthy, but most peoples' first thought when they hear the name "Bobby Knight" is his temper. Images of him arguing with the referees or throwing a chair seem to be the first response people have to him. The boss with a low boiling point might engender fear and/or a distorted type of respect, but he or she does not foster loyalty or teamwork.

8. Negativity: In its most pronounced form, negativity creates a culture of doom and dread. The joy and spark of one's work soon flee under an onslaught of negativism. When a leader allows himself or herself to be ruled by a spirit of negativism, the result is to post a large "Do Not Disturb" sign on his or her door. The flow of ideas diminishes, and a team soon becomes little more than a task force: get the job done and move on.

9. Withholding information: Occasionally leaders fall into the trap of withholding information as a way of controlling who has the power and influence. Sometimes this is intentional, but just as often it is a subtle and unrecognized pattern. Unfortunately, this behavior generally has the opposite effect than what is intended. Those on the outside listening in, those who are kept at a distance by not being given key information do not respond with added respect for those in the know. They generally respond with feelings of distrust.

10. Failing to give proper recognition: Leaders who have to have all the limelight soon find themselves standing alone. Corporate and organizational cultures thrive on shared recognition, and it is particularly powerful when the CEO takes time to shine the light on others. Dale Carnegie, the master teacher for a generation of American leaders, said that the two sweetest words in all the world are a person's first and last name. To hear your name spoken in recognition of a job well done is transformative. And the opposite is just as true. When a leader fails to recognize the person who performs well and/or goes the second mile, not only does the entire organization miss a feel-good, do-it-again moment, but the person involved also feels ignored, underappreciated, and disrespected. His or her desire to reach the goal again begins to diminish.

11. Claiming credit for work done by others: Corporate culture and *esprit de corps* is also negatively impacted when senior leaders claim sole credit for work done by others. In every public report to the board or the faculty and staff, I look for ways to give credit where credit is due, and whenever possible I name names rather than just express blanket appreciation.

12. Making excuses: Leaders, of all people, must not make excuses. There will be reasons and explanations as to why projects don't succeed or one's personal performance falls short, but there is no excuse for a pattern of making excuses. Leaders have to take responsibility for their actions. When we stop making excuses, not only does our performance improve but also our interpersonal relations.

13. Clinging to the past: Several years ago I flew from Chicago to Kansas City for a corporate board meeting. I was met at the KC airport by a nice young man who had been sent by the company to drive me to the hotel where the meeting was to take place. Leaving the airport, we began the usual casual conversation that accompanies such trips. As we talked, I noticed that the driver was constantly looking in the rearview mirror, as if we were being followed or he was watching something in particular.

I finally asked him why he kept looking in the rearview mirror. "Oh, it's nothing really," he said. "It's just that last year I was hit from behind by another car." While I certainly understood the traumatic nature of such an accident, I had to wonder how long he will drive looking backward rather than looking forward.

Leaders certainly must have a sense of history—personal and corporate—but the focus of one's work must be forward. The successes or failures of the past are past. Period. We learn from them, and we glance back from time to time; but renewal comes from setting our sights on the next thing rather than the last thing.

14. Playing favorites: Leaders who retain the confidence of those with whom they work are careful to treat everyone with the same level of respect and fairness. If a perception develops that some are treated with undue deference or that the rules and expectations are not consistent throughout the organization, the well of goodwill is tainted and leaves a bad taste, and a bitter spirit sets in.

15. Refusal to express regret or offer a sincere apology: This can also undermine a leader's effectiveness over time. It can be a bit humbling to go to a coworker, particularly one you supervise, and offer an apology. But there is magic in such moments. Relationships and mutual respect are strengthened, and loyalty is enhanced rather than diminished.

16. Not listening: On the part of senior leadership, this is one of the most common complaints. "He hears but doesn't really listen." When leaders fail to listen, they not only restrict the funnel of feedback—they also send forth "an armada of negative messages."[7] A deaf ear speaks loudly, saying, "I don't care. I'm not really interested in you or what you have to say," and so on. When we fail to be interested in others and what they have to say, they quickly fail to be interested in *us* or what *we* have to say.

17. Failing to express gratitude: This is a missed opportunity. The power of a simple thank you, spoken or jotted down in a handwritten note, can hardly be overestimated.

18. Punishing the messenger: Feedback, honest assessment, hard facts, and clear data are vital for leadership decisions. To keep the channels open, one must separate the message from the messenger. When I was elected president of Olivet, we were already living next to the campus and knew most of the faculty and staff as friends. On the night of the election, as the first shock waves began to fade, my wife, Jill, said to me, "I'm afraid that no one will tell us the truth anymore." She feared that now that our relationship had suddenly shifted from "friends" to the "boss" and the "boss's wife," people would tell us only what they thought we wanted to hear. I replied, "That's a good point—I think it will depend on us. We have to maintain openness so that people will know they can trust us to respond as appropriately to complaints as to compliments."

19. Passing the buck: "Passing the buck is one of those terrifying hybrid flaws. Take a healthy dose of *needing to win* and *making excuses*. Mix it with *refusing to apologize* and *failing to give proper recognition*. Sprinkle in a faint hint of *punish the messenger* and *getting angry*. What you end up with is passing the buck, blaming others for our mistakes."[8]

20. An excessive need to be "me": This is Goldsmith's final fatal flaw. It occurs when a leader excuses his or her faults or gives himself or herself excessive liberty based solely on the perception that *It's just me being me. That's the way I am* or *I have that right because I am the boss*. The remedy is simple: less *me* coupled with more of *them* equals success.

Fortunately, most leaders have only to address a few of these flaws. As a leader, one needs to identify which three or four flaws might possibly be part of his or her pattern of relationships. The good news is that any of these habits can be corrected.

FROM ENEMY TO FRIEND

During the American Revolution a Baptist pastor named Peter Miller enjoyed the friendship of George Washington. One of his neighbors was an angry and difficult fellow named Michael Widman. Widman did all he could to oppose and even humiliate the pastor. One day Widman was arrested for treason and sentenced to die. In response, Pastor Peter Miller traveled seventy miles on foot to Philadelphia to plead for the life of the traitor.

"No, Peter," General Washington said. "I cannot grant you the life of your friend."

"My friend?" exclaimed the old preacher. "He's the bitterest enemy I have."

"What?" replied Washington, "You've walked seventy miles to save the life of an enemy? That puts the matter in different light. I'll grant your pardon."

And he did. Peter Miller then took Michael Widman back home—no longer an enemy but a friend.[9]

DYSFUNCTIONAL SYSTEMS

Over time, not only relationships but also systems and work habits can deteriorate. An organization might be doing the same things that worked in the past, but now those same procedures and processes do not yield the same results. Because of this natural entropy, leaders must not assume that all is well. Effective organizations regularly evaluate how their standard operating practices are doing.

This is done formally through tests and measurements of the raw data. For example, at Olivet we established a highly organized and integrated recruitment system for our traditional undergraduate enrollment. As the pieces were put into place, enrollment began to climb, resulting in a ten-year streak of steady increases. Then suddenly one fall, having done what we had done every other year, we saw a drop in freshmen enrollment.

Was this an anomaly, just one of those things? Was there some external variant that had negatively impacted our enrollment? Or was it time to carefully review what and why we were doing what we had been doing? Whatever the reason, we needed to correct or compensate for it. A drop in freshmen enrollment one year is significant, for a school lives with that for the next four years. But what is particularly important is to ensure that the one-year experience is not repeated and does not become a pattern. That can be disastrous.

As we analyzed the data and reviewed, step by step, our normal processes, we discovered that in the early fall, the year before the decline, we had delayed an important mailing that awards an initial conditional financial aid amount to a prospective student even before he or she applies for admission. This technique is designed to encourage prospective students to take a serious look at Olivet and to complete the application process. By delaying a mailing, we inadvertently lost a window of opportunity and narrowed, by default, the size of the enrollment funnel. Fewer students in the process meant fewer students enrolled.

The reasons for the delay all made sense at the time, but with the unintended consequences that followed, we quickly repaired the processes and built into the system a level of safeguards and a measure of redundancy to help ensure that we would not have that experience again. One best not wait until it is pouring to fix the roof—do it at the first sign of rain.

7

RE
LEASE

*Take the first step in faith. You don't have
to see the whole staircase—just take the first step.*
—Martin Luther King Jr.

*Life is not a dress rehearsal. Stop practicing what you're going to do
and just go do it. In one bold stroke you can transform today.*
—Marilyn Grey

A vital part of the re-vision process is to for the leader to come to the place at which he or she can let go of things that are no longer effective. The freedom to lead is enhanced when one breaks from a paralysis that can set in over time as one does the same kinds of things again and again. There is sense of emancipation when organizations begin to do new things in new ways. A new energy comes with the prospect of new accomplishments. But release does not come without a measure of anxiety.

Most people are fascinated by trapeze artists, those daring individuals who fly through the air with the greatest of ease. One thing to note is that they always work in teams. The person called the *flyer* climbs a narrow set of steps straight up, high above the crowd, where he or she mounts a tiny platform and grasps the crossbar of a trapeze.

When the time is right, the flyer leaps from the platform, swinging out through the air, using his or her body for momentum. Little by little the flyer moves back and forth with increasing speed and height. In contrast, the catcher hangs from his or her knees on another trapeze with hands free, ready to reach out.

The moment of truth comes when the flyer lets go of the trapeze and sails into the air with no support, no guarantees, and no connection to the earth. In those brief moments, just before gravity takes over, the flyer often does a somersault or maybe two. Imagine what it is like for that person to be in the middle of a somersault out over the crowd. Hold that image in your mind for a moment. Within that frame you see this person whirling through the air with absolutely nothing to keep him or her from ultimately plunging to his or her death.

What do you suppose that feels like? Do you think the flyer feels more fully alive than at any other time—every cell and nerve ending on edge? Is that individual feeling exhilarated, terrified, or both? In the next moment, as we "unfreeze" the frame, the catcher swings into view. He has been timing his arcs perfectly. He arrives just as the flyer loses momentum and is beginning to descend. His hands clasp the arms of the flyer, just in the nick of time.

The flyer, of course, cannot see the catcher; to the flyer everything is a blur. But just when it is most critically needed, the flyer is suddenly snatched out of the air and carried home by the momentum of the catcher. Wow! I can't imagine what that is really like—to let go of everything and trust that some unseen set of hands out there somewhere will catch and carry me to safety. Talk about faith overcoming doubt!

Long-term leaders and the organizations with which they work may often have to let go of some long-held patterns and practices before they can take hold of the next project or program. There is risk, but there is also energy and reward when one learns to release.

Most organizations are over-managed and under-led.[1] Management deals with the ability to cope with complexity and problem-solving. Leadership is mainly about change, and change calls for letting go and taking hold of the next new thing. Leaders who re-vision their work and their organizations are risk-takers. Their risks are not reckless or thoughtless; in fact, they are generally well-planned and well-executed strategies. Even so, there is still an element of risk as one releases the past to grab onto the future.

John Kotter makes an insightful observation as he writes about the distinction between aligning people versus organizing and staffing. "To executives who are overeducated in management and undereducated in leadership, the idea of getting people moving in the same direction appears to be an organizational problem. What executives need to do, however, is not organize people but align them."[2]

Alignment has more to do with direction than organization. Its energy stems from vision and strategy rather than systems and structure. Thus, part of the leadership challenge is to communicate effectively the next things—projects, goals, targets—so that individuals throughout the organization are aligned toward those things. With clear goals, individuals are better able to release, to let go of the practices and perceptions of the past.

One of the features of this idea of alignment versus organization is that alignment carries with it an empowering dimension that organization alone cannot deliver. "One of the reasons some organizations have difficulty adjusting to rapid changes is that so many people in those companies feel relatively powerless."[3]

However, once people know with clarity where the organization is headed and how their work fits into that grand scheme, they become much more effective and confident that what they do and how they do their work will make a significant difference. They begin to fly.

TRUST

I spend a lot of time on airplanes. I've noticed that once the plane is loaded with passengers and fuel, the captain takes it to the far end of a long runway, and for a moment we pause. The seatbelts are fastened, the seat backs are "in the full and upright position," the tray-tables are up, cell phones are off, and most of the causal chatter is suspended. The pilot checks the instrument panel one last time.

When the signal is given from the control tower, the pilot releases the brakes and pushes the throttle forward. The plane begins to move faster, then faster and faster. Finally, when the groundspeed is sufficient, the wings are adjusted to increase lift—and suddenly the plane is airborne.

We take this all for granted; but remember: halfway down the runway, with the engines fully engaged and the plane quickly gaining speed toward the end of the runway, the plane is still not flying. Pilots and passengers alike have learned to hold steady, not panic, keep the plane pointed in the right direction, keep the engines fully engaged, and then, when the moment is right, the pilot pulls on the yoke and the plane suddenly lifts off. The new begins as one lets go of the old.

WELCOME—NOW PLEASE GO AWAY

Jill and I were walking through Harvard Square one afternoon when we first saw it. It was very clever. We were in Cambridge, Massachusetts, that fall just as university students were arriving from all over the world to study at Harvard or Radcliff or down the street at MIT, the Massachusetts Institute of Technology.

As we walked the streets, getting the lay of the land, popping in and out of bookstores and coffee shops and taking in the other sights of that rather eclectic place, it was Jill who spotted the sign first. "Look at that," she said. I turned to see a large, well-lit sign in the window of a travel agency. It read, "Welcome—Now Please Go Away."

We stood there for a few moments taking in the message. The unwritten subtext of this sign was twofold. First, the message was a recognition that almost everyone walking those streets was from somewhere else and thus would be traveling back home at fall break or at the end of the semester or taking other kinds of trips along the way; and the travel agency, of course, wanted to help them "go away" by booking tickets and making travel plans.

But there was, at least to me, more than a mercenary implication to the sign. For in a way it was also saying, "We are glad you are here, but we know in reality that you are just passing through. This university-town is just one stop on your lifetime journey. You are here, but at the same time you are 'on your way' to the future, to professions and personal lives that will take you beyond the streets and structures of Harvard Square." What was true for those students is true for leaders and organizations. Each is, or should be, continually moving on to the next stage—the next part of the journey.

One important step in taking the next step in the re-visioning process is taking stock of where the organization and its leader are at any given moment. Most people are familiar with the maps in shopping malls or amusement parks that say, "You are here." Those signs exist to orient individuals who are in unfamiliar territory. They help one determine where he or she is in comparison to where he or she may wish to go, showing how to get there.

There is a sense that as an organization and its leader re-visions, there need to be moments along the way when three questions are answered:

Where are you?

Where do you want to go?

How will you get there?

Confronting those questions and coming to a clear answer have a way of breaking the hold of inertia that keeps organizations from increased productivity and development. Clarity on those issues also energizes a leader and releases him or her to chart a new course. Having a set of goals in life gives one both focus and direction. Goals provide a framework through which to determine what can be released and what must be continued.

For more than thirty years Jill and I have spent New Year's Eve with the same two couples. Regardless of where we were living or whatever else was going on in life, we have met for a few days over the New Year's holiday. Each year as our time together comes to an end, we gather around a table to talk about the past year and think together about the year to come. As those conversations wind down, each person is given a piece of paper to write out the high points of that particular New Year's Eve together.

Then we make predictions for the coming year. For example, in an election year we may each predict who we think will be the presidential candidates and who will be elected, or the state of the economy, or personal predictions concerning someone in the group. A third part of the written activity is to write down our personal goals for the new year. We reminisce. We predict. And then we set goals.

After finishing our writings, those sheets are sealed in envelopes. Then we open last year's envelopes and read aloud our remembrances and our predictions and our goals from a year ago. Since we have been doing this for so long, we now also open the envelopes from ten years ago and twenty years ago. What is most interesting to me is to hear the goals that were set by each of us at different points in our lives and to take stock of how those goals have shaped us.

Over time a person's goals—personal, professional, and spiritual—set the direction for his or her life. In the end the direction of one's life helps determine his or her destiny. Standing before a locator map in a shopping mall and noticing the "You are here" sticker has value only in relationship to where you want to go. It doesn't make much difference where you are if you have no idea where you want to go. However, once you know and accept where you are and determine where you want to go, then you can decide how to get there.

There are some individuals who look at the map of their lives, and the map tells them, "You are here," but for whatever reason, they don't accept the answer. They resist the truth and block it out. They don't face reality.

I had a roommate when I was in college who was a terrific guy. He was funny, well liked, a fine athlete, and certainly bright enough to do college work—but he just couldn't deal with reality. He said he wanted to be in college, that he wanted to graduate and become a teacher and coach. But he didn't focus. He drifted. He assumed that he would somehow get by, as he had done from time to time in other situations.

But ultimately the only direction one who is drifting can go is down. And that is what happened to my friend; he didn't take time to seriously take stock of where he was in relationship to where he wanted to go. He lost track of where he was academically and spiritually and finally dropped out of school, never to finish college. He never became a teacher or a coach.

One cannot drift his or her way to the top. Goals are not reached by accident. They must be pursued step by step, day by day. In the midst of a process of re-visioning, leaders must evaluate whether there is a clear and honest sense of where they are today.

When I was in graduate school, I worked for a time as a sales associate in a fine men's department store. Twice a year we closed the store early to take inventory. We counted every item on every shelf and in every storeroom. This was before the days of computers and bar-coding that provides continuous monitoring for inventory control now. What we did was tedious work, and it was costly, in a way, for the store. We were all getting paid, but we weren't selling anything during those hours. Nonetheless, we did it twice a year. The merchants who ran the store knew the importance of taking stock—of knowing for sure where they were.

JUGGLING 101

Not long ago I picked up a most interesting book, *Lessons from the Art of Juggling*. It's an instruction book on how to learn to juggle, but it is more than that, as the subtitle suggests: *How to Achieve Your Full Potential in Business, Learning and Life.*[4] The book, of course, is built around the metaphor of juggling. It begins with an opening poem.

I,
Juggler,
Stand between two spheres.
The expression
Of my Enlightened thoughts
Goes out
And up
To the Sun.
The soles
And balls
Of my feet

Hug the loam of the Earth,
As I weave the dancing patterns of Infinity.

Deeply, I am a juggler,
I breathe out into the Universe
I have breathed
In

I . . .
Juggle
And
Am
Juggled.[5]

The thought that captured my attention is this: "I . . . juggle and am juggled."

As leaders, juggling is more than a metaphor; it is a way of life. A leader's life is multidimensional and constantly in motion. Leaders are called upon daily to juggle work, social life, family responsibilities, physical health, attitudes, actions, reactions, and work-related issues and relationships.

We juggle . . . and we are juggled.

Juggling suggests the need for synchronization, harmonious rhythms, and keeping a certain overall situational awareness. One cannot juggle and be distracted—and yet one learns to juggle almost subconsciously. There develops an inner focus. One of the secrets to juggling is to stay centered, that is, to stay focused and balanced. One can do a lot of things *at once* if he or she stays centered. And what is true of juggling is true in life as well.

THE THINGS THEY CARRIED

Each year the City of Chicago chooses a "book of the year" as a means of fostering literary thought and discussion throughout the city. The book is read in the public schools, talked about in the cultural circles of the area, promoted in various means, and critiqued at the city's colleges and universities.

The book selected a few years ago was *The Things They Carried*, by award-winning writer Tim O'Brien. It is a collection of inter-related stories and essays set in the midst of the Vietnam War. In the first chapter O'Brien introduces the reader to a cast of characters who reappear throughout the rest of the book. He introduces them to us by describing "the things they carried" as a metaphor for life in general. For example,

> First Lieutenant Jimmy Cross carried letters from a girl named Martha, a junior at Mount Sebastian College in New Jersey. They were not love letters, but Lieutenant Cross was hoping, so he kept them folded in plastic at the bottom of his rucksack. In the late afternoon, after a day's march, he would dig his foxhole, wash his hands under a canteen, unwrap the letters, hold them with the tips of his fingers, and spend the last hour of light pretending.[6]

> The things they carried were largely determined by necessity. Among the necessities or near-necessities were P-38 can openers, pocket knives, heat tabs, wrist watches, dog tags, mosquito repellent, chewing gum, candy, cigarettes, salt tablets, packets of Kool-Aid, lighters, matches, sewing kits, military payment certificates, C-rations, and two or three canteens of water. Together, these items weighed between fifteen and twenty pounds, depending upon a man's habits or rate of metabolism.[7]

> Kiowa, a devout Baptist, carried an illustrated New Testament that had been presented to him by his father, who taught Sunday School in Oklahoma City. As a hedge against bad times, however, Kiowa also carried his grandmother's distrust of the white man and his grandfather's old hunting hatchet.[8]

Because the land was mined and booby-trapped, it was standard operating procedure for each man to carry a steel-centered, nylon-covered flak jacket, which weighed 6.7 pounds, but which on hot days seemed much heavier . . . [and] because you could die so quickly, each man carried at least one large compress bandage, usually in the helmet band for easy access.

Because the nights were cold, and because the monsoons were wet, each carried a green plastic poncho that could be used as a raincoat or groundsheet or makeshift tent. With its quilted liner, the poncho weighed almost two pounds, but it was worth every ounce.

They carried all the emotional baggage of men who might die. Grief, terror, love, longing—these were intangibles, but the intangibles had their own mass and specific gravity, they had tangible weight. They carried their own lives. The pressures were enormous. They shared the weight of memory. They took up what others could no longer bear. By and large they carried these things inside, maintaining the masks of composure. And often, they carried each other, the wounded or weak.[9]

Tim O'Brien's image of a person carrying various things as he moves through the demands of life and death is a metaphor worth thinking about. I have watched people come and go from the university for decades. I see freshmen arrive each fall, seniors leave each spring, and I see those who return to campus at graduation or homecoming. A freshman arrives on campus carrying hopes and dreams and aspirations, but he or she also carries a measure of anxiety packed into some corner of a suitcase or a book bag. Seniors leave carrying plenty of memories and lots of lessons learned—some of them in class. They carry with them a new set of hopes and dreams and some new angst as well. Alumni arrive as those who linger in front of a mirror. They represent different years, different decades, different stages of life.

In O'Brien's book the individuals are defined by what they carried—and so are we. We are all defined to some degree by what we carry, what we refuse to carry, and what we cast away. The choice to carry it or to lay it aside is a decision we make with many of the things we pick up over time. And we do pick up things along the way. This is particularly true for leaders who continue to serve in the same place over many years.

We pick up responsibilities, influence, and authority. We carry added financial pressures and sometimes a health issue. Over time we gain added relationships, successes, and failures. We carry memories, scars, and lots of incidental cares and worries.

Sometimes our hopes and dreams get replaced with disappointment, even disillusionment, and suddenly—yet not so suddenly—we find that we are burdened down by "the things we carry." If leaders are to remain effective, they must find ways from time to time to let go of some things that weigh them down. And we must also let go of the failures and shortcomings of our co-workers. We can't move forward together without this.

I learned a powerful set of lessons late one night when I was a teenager. I ran away from home when I was fifteen. It still embarrasses me to think about it. Some rather incidental disagreement with my folks made me think I was old enough to just strike out on my own. As I remember, I had about forty dollars saved up from mowing lawns, which seemed like a lot of money at the time.

So after school, with that money burning a hole in my pocket and a sense of independence and adolescent rebellion stirring in my mind, I bought a bus ticket from my little town in western Ohio to Dayton, Ohio. From there I bought a ticket to Indianapolis, and it was just after I boarded that bus to Indy that I realized I had made a mistake—but how do you go back?

It was almost midnight by the time I reached Indianapolis. There was no one there to meet me, no place to stay, and my forty dollars were now twenty-something. My parents had no idea where I was—I had just not come home from school.

Finally, I called them from a pay phone. That conversation is burned into my mind.

"John, is that you?" my father said when he heard my voice.

"Yes."

"Where are you?"

"Indianapolis"

"How did you get there?"

"On the bus"

"Are you okay?"

"Yes—no, I want to come home."

"Sure," he said.

I bought a ticket for a bus that was leaving for Dayton within the next few minutes.

About two and a half hours later, when I stepped off that bus in the middle of the night, there were my mother and my father waiting. It was my mother who set the tone. No harsh words, no stern looks or angry gestures; there was rejoicing, with hugs and kisses. That's not what I deserved, but it's what I needed.

It was a moment of grace. It was a good moment. It was a God moment. And perhaps the most remarkable thing about that event was that my parents never mentioned it again—ever. Their ability and willingness to let it go empowered me to let it go as well. I was released from the guilt and embarrassment and was enabled to move on with a renewed vision of my future.

That boyhood experience illustrates the power of letting go of moments that if held onto could create a climate and perhaps a trajectory that is counterproductive. My parents had every right to impose some strict punishment, but rather than making that episode a defining moment in my adolescence, they released it. They either consciously or intuitively chose, in those dark early hours, not to allow it to become more than it was. They let it go, and as a result the moment became a positive moment, which changed my view of home, my parents, and myself.

Re-vision in one's life and organization can be enhanced as long-term leaders periodically release the accumulated baggage that naturally occurs over time in the running of a company and within the matrix of complex business and personal relationships. Remember—the trapeze artist has to master the art of letting go before he or she takes hold of what comes next.

Edison failed many times in his various attempts to create an incandescent light, yet he would not be defined by those moments of failure. He released the failure and took with him the experience of what didn't work as he moved on to his next attempt to find what would work. He was able to re-vision a world where darkness could be controlled by incorporating the lessons learned from failure. This ability to learn and adapt in the face of failure or disappointment provides leaders with a critical advantage.

Leadership cannot flourish without a positive attitude regarding learning and mistakes. Successful organizations and the individuals who lead them are able to fail without failing. Thomas Watson, founder of IBM, said, "If you want to succeed, double your failure rate."[10]

8

RE
FRESH

Whatever you do or dream you can do—begin it. Boldness has genius and power and magic in it. Don't worry about being worried. You're heading out on an adventure, and you can always change your mind along the way and try something else.

—Tracy Kidder

During the 2012 United States presidential campaign *The New Yorker* ran a feature article on candidate Mitt Romney. At one point the article described a conversation that he had about his view of business. Noting that Romney's father, George Romney, had been the chief executive officer of American Motors Corporation, the interviewer asked why General Motors Corporation, which for years was the most successful car company in the world, had fallen into bankruptcy and decline. Romney responded,

> My dad had a statement he would make that proved to be true in this industry, as in all others. I remember as a boy saying to him, "Dad, we make the best cars, don't we?" And he said yes. And I said, "Then why don't we sell the most cars?" And he said, "Well, someday we may." And he said, "Because,

Mitt"—and this is his quote—"there's nothing as vulnerable as entrenched success." And the auto industry, in particular General Motors, was so successful for so long that it didn't recognize the need to innovate, to become more productive, to become more efficient, or it would ultimately be vulnerable to foreign competition.

A successful company could have low costs, it could make a better product, and it could have a highly profitable run. But if companies become complacent, in my dad's lexicon, they could become more vulnerable . . . there's nothing as vulnerable as entrenched success.[1]

That section of the article went on to point out that, "there are some enterprises that have found that they can, despite their huge success, reinvigorate themselves, reinvent themselves, and maintain their lead. G.E. did that under Jack Welch."[2]

For re-visioning to take hold, organizations must be periodically refreshed with new ideas, new approaches, and new energy. This is true for successful as well as struggling organizations. The root systems that nurture and sustain organizations need to be well-tended.

IT WAS HUMOROUS AND NOT SO HUMOROUS

Several years ago, not long after the construction of the Benner Library and Resource Center at Olivet, the university decided to create a campus "quad" between the library and Ludwig Center. It was then, and remains today, the most heavily traveled spot on campus. A generous gift was received from an alumni family named Decker, and soon the work began to transform this barren space into "The Decker Quad."

The shape at the center of the quad was designed as a large "O" with the names of senior class presidents and student council presidents to be placed around the brick walkway. Plantings were added to enhance the beauty of the area, and collegiate benches were distributed throughout the quad. The sidewalks were expanded, and there was a small stage area at the south end to facilitate student and campus gatherings.

All these features were important parts of the plan; but the heart of the entire project was right in the middle of a large, raised area bordered with brick and stone. There, with great pageantry, the university planted the Olivet Nazarene University "Tree of Learning." It is then that the story turned funny—and not funny.

Within a few weeks following the dedication of the quad and the planting of the tree, its leaves began to discolor and soon fall away. The revered "Tree of Learning," which was to be a living symbol of learning, died. That is never a good thing—for the tree of learning to die on a university campus. Very quickly, without fanfare, the dead tree was uprooted and replaced with a healthy new sapling. Once again, little by little, the new tree also began to wane, and it, too, died.

Jokes soon followed. "Did you hear that the tree of learning keeps dying at Olivet?"

Soon the university, with the help of a good horticulturist, diagnosed the problem. There weren't sufficient soil and proper drainage for the roots of the tree to sink deeply into the ground below the now "paved and bricked" lawn. The tree simply could not flourish without strong roots. So once more, with renewed vigor and enhanced understanding, a new tree was planted in an improved soil base. Sure enough, once the root system began to spread down and out, the tree flourished. Learning was once again alive and well at Olivet.

The tree in the quad is a living metaphor of organizational life, as well as life in general. Like trees, organizations, as well as individuals, must have strong and healthy root systems if they are to thrive. Often in the life of an organization there comes a time when the soil needs to be freshened and the root systems nourished. I have experienced that cycle a few times at the university.

I HAVE DECIDED TO GET A TATTOO

A couple of years ago I decided that it was time to begin a campus-wide conversation about those elements that set the school apart from other universities. My goal was to refresh our self-image and our ways of talking about the effectiveness of what we do. I introduced the concept with a speech entitled "The Marks of an Olivetian." The speech began with this poem.

I have decided to get a tattoo
It just seems like the "in" thing to do.
Some may think it quite bold
My choice of purple and gold
To emblaze on my chest—ONU.

But
I see nothing taboo 'bout the art of tattoo
And no reason to not follow through,
Though a few will remark,
"He's now missed the mark,
With his devotion to old ONU."

True,
I may wish to complain, when I first feel the pain,
But I know when the artist is through,
That I'll be proud to declare,
On my chest that is bare,
My commitment to thee—ONU.

Most will agree that the term "tattoo artist" is an oxymoron; nonetheless, as most people know, tattooing has become a very popular practice in the last few years, particularly among university students. When I was growing up, a tattoo was commonly identified with bikers or inmates or the occasional sailor back from the war who couldn't quite remember how he got a tattoo. By the time I was in college, the practice had expanded to include heavy-metal rock band members and hippies.

But all that has changed. These days, having a tattoo is very "in" and does not necessarily carry with it a negative impression. However, this renewed popularity of tattooing is still hard for many of my generation to understand. It needles us to see young men and women permanently marking their bodies. It gets "under our skin" a bit. But even so, its popularity continues.

There are many reasons, I suppose, that people choose to have a tattoo. In some cultures it is related to specific rites of passage. In the United States, however, having a tattoo simply seems to be a way of expressing one's individuality or indicating affinity with a particular group or way of life. And, of course, the number-one reason among college students for tattoos is—to annoy parents.

Organizations and the individuals who lead them will often bear the marks of their shared history. If one is to help an organization re-vision its identity and its future, a leader may need to refresh the symbols and signs that bear witness to the life and vitality of an organization. Organizations, and the people who populate and lead them, can get stale over time. The marks of fatigue begin to appear, and soon apathy replaces enthusiasm. There can be the appearance and perception of progress without anything new or substantial really taking place within the life of the organization.

SHALL WE, TOO, LOOK TO THE FUTURE WITH OPTIMISM?

A couple of years ago I began my annual State of the University address with the following story.

It was a slow day in the town of Worthington, and streets were deserted. Times were tough. It seemed everyone was living on credit and was therefore in debt. A tourist visiting the area drove through town and stopped at the Do Drop Inn, the only motel in the area.

The stranger laid a one-hundred-dollar bill on the desk, saying to the manager that he wanted to inspect the rooms upstairs to select one for the night. As soon as the man walked upstairs, the motel owner grabbed the bill and ran next door to pay his debt to the butcher.

The butcher took the $100 and handed it immediately to a farmer who was just dropping off an order of beef that had been purchased on credit. The farmer, in turn, took the $100 and headed down the street to pay his bill at the local Co-op.

The fellow at the Co-op took the money and paid his fore-man the $100 he owed him in back pay. Immediately, the fore-man slipped out the back door to quickly settle his debt to a certain local—what shall we say—"lady of the evening," so to speak, who had also been facing hard times.

The "lady" then rushed immediately to the motel and paid off her room bill. The proprietor then placed the $100 back on the counter just as the traveler came down the stairs, stating that the rooms were not satisfactory. He then picked up the $100 bill and left town.

No one produced anything.

No one earned anything.

And yet everyone's net worth improved.

The whole town is now out of debt and, therefore, looks to the future with renewed optimism.

Some organizations are like that. They remain busy and seem-ingly productive, but in the final analysis nothing of lasting value has accrued. Most leaders live and work in a world of mixed mes-sages. In such an environment it is often difficult to find meaningful ways to refresh an organization with new prospects and plans for the future.

ANALYSIS OF ASCENT

In reflecting on the nearly unparalleled success of Elon University, George Keller identified a series of strategies used to refresh the vision and focus of the university. First among them is the fostering of an overarching commitment to a culture of quality. The most obvious, although not the most significant, evidence of this is the fine campus at Elon. The campus provides an example of the maxim "First we shape our buildings—then they shape us." Many organizations would experience a wave of renewal if they simply took better care of their facilities.

But the commitment to quality does not end with the manicured lawns, flowerbeds, and fountains. Quality must show up at the core of each program and in the work of every individual. One of the Olivet staff members who toured Elon told me of a conversation he had with a groundskeeper who was tending one of the flower beds. As they began to visit, the Olivet staff member said to the fellow from Elon, "Tell me about your job."

Without hesitation the fellow said, "I recruit students."

This individual understood that the quality of his work was part of the overall mission of the university, and it ultimately made a difference as prospective students toured the campus. Such a culture is contagious.

A second aspect that gave rise to Elon's transformation is the school's addiction to planning. The simple process of casting a vision, setting goals, and communicating each next step on the journey cannot be overlooked. In his fine book *Leading Change*, John Kotter has an interesting section he calls, "Planning Versus Praying for Results."[3]

Kotter suggests that too often planning is too general and vague and therefore tentative both in its detail and expectations. "We are going to grow" or "We are going to have a first-rate academic general education program" are not plans—they are only wishes, hopes, and prayers. He notes that part of the planning process must include some strategies for quick performance improvements. The short-term win brings energy and signals that change is underway. He writes, "People don't just hope and pray for performance improvements. They plan for short-term wins, organize accordingly, and implement the plan to make things happen."[4]

This seems simple, yet this failure to start undercuts the transformation process from the beginning. Kotter suggests that there are three reasons that leaders and managers fall short at this point. One reason is the press of the daily demands leaders must also respond to. Thus tyranny of the urgent suppresses the energy, time, and desire it takes to start something new. This can be countered by clarifying the vision and clearly—overly, perhaps—communicating to those involved in implementation the specifics of the next steps to take. The vision is the compass; the plan must be the map.

Another reason organizations falter at the start of a new plan is a lack of confidence or understanding that major change can and does start with a few small steps. It's the "What difference will that make?" attitude.

A third element that undermines the move to added quality and efficient and effective service is lack of sufficient management. "To a large degree, leadership deals with the long term and management with the immediate future. Without enough good management, the planning, organizing, and controlling for results will not be sufficient."[5] In contract to this possibility, at Elon everyone got on board quickly, and things began to change for the better, and this created an appetite for more.

In the final analysis leaders don't lead businesses or organizations—we lead people. Thus, the selection, training, and rewarding of people are essential. It is the Jim Collins idea of getting the right people on the bus and then making sure they are all in the right seats. This idea was paramount in the re-visioning and renewal of Elon and has created a winsome culture of inclusion and community. It's part of what some have called the "Elon Way," in which people are encouraged to be polite and service-oriented. I recall on one of my visits to Elon hearing a few of the senior staff talk about the campus-wide commitment to "speak and smile." Throughout my visit I couldn't keep from noticing that nearly everyone I met on the walkways or in the buildings would smile and say, "Hello."

This aspect of the university culture has contributed to a very small turnover rate among faculty and staff. Rather than coming and going, people come and stay, thus providing continuity and strength for the key elements of the campus ethos.

An additional factor to the ascent has been Elon's willingness to create "a distinctive niche in the crowded firmament of American colleges and universities."[6] There is a freedom that comes when a school or organization ceases trying to be all things to all people. Elon's growth began when it narrowed its focus to a particular incoming student profile. They were not ready to compete head to head with the elites but did believe they could attract the strong student who may have just missed acceptance at Davidson or Duke.

A fifth aspect that has enabled the re-visioning of Elon to become reality is the financial acumen of the board and senior leadership. Pricing, tuition discounting, creative financing, strong development efforts, willingness to borrow, and careful management have provided much of the fuel necessary for growth and development. "Elon has been both daring and inventive and yet prudent and scrupulous. It has leveraged its limited funds with remarkable skill."[7]

A final characteristic of the new Elon has been its tenacious and very effective marketing efforts. The leadership at Elon understands that effective marketing is more than advertising and promotion. Marketing for the university rests on five pillars: program, price, place, people, and promotion. The school has sought to develop a solid academic, athletic, and student life *program* that is attractive and rewarding for its target audience. Elon strategically sets its *price*—tuition, fees, room and board—just below that of most of its rivals, creating a sense of value. The strong emphasis on campus beatification has created an attractive *place* for living and learning. Elon's *people* embrace the mission and are hired and trained to embody the values and culture of the school. With those things in place, a skillful program of *promotion* was initiated to target media, publishers of college guides, the wider high education community, alumni, government leaders, and most of all, prospective students and their families.

These factors—a commitment to quality, an addition to planning, an emphasis on the importance of people, a willingness to define its niche, steady financial acumen, and its rising skill in marketing and branding—have been the rungs of the ladder that make it possible for a sleepy, little-known, not-highly-regarded college to become a rising star among a cadre of small, somewhat elite universities across the country.

Leaders have been and still can be catalytic in refreshing the vision, self-awareness, and openness to new ideas and possibilities. Elon University is one example; there are many more. When each story of a given organization is carefully unpacked, it becomes clear that it all started with a single voice, an individual who sees what others failed to see and in so doing was also able to articulate the vision and enlist others to join in the quest of a preferred future.

At times leaders who live and work amid the never-ending tension between what must be done and what should be done should see themselves as Captain Jack Sparrow of the widely popular *Pirates of the Caribbean* movies, standing tall at the very front of the ship with the wind and spray in his face. Looking forward, he shouts to everyone on board that now-famous line from the final scene of *Pirates of the Caribbean: The Curse of the Black Pearl:* "Now bring me that horizon!"

Leaders are men and women of the horizon—looking out there into the future, standing on tiptoes, leaning forward, faces pressed toward the glass to catch a glimpse beyond the now. The task of helping refresh one's work and life is embedded in the ability to see something new. Once they see the future, others begin to see it as well. Vision carries with it a magnetic power. Daniel Burnham, the great Chicago architect, said it well: "Make no little plans; they have no magic to stir men's blood."[8]

Successful leaders also understand the importance of managing the mood of their organizations. This ability is closely linked to the concept of emotional intelligence. Effective executives are self-aware and empathetic. They can stay in touch with their own emotions while intuitively grasping how others feel. Thus, leaders are like an orchestra conductor. A conductor's authority rests on two things: the orchestra's confidence in his or her knowledge of the whole score and the conductor's connection with the individual musicians.

Edward Hallowell has written an interesting article titled "The Human Moment at Work."[9] The thrust of the article is that in recent years with the advent of e-mail, texting, video conferencing, and so on there is the danger of leaders losing what he calls the human moment: an authentic encounter that can happen only when two people share the same physical space. "I have given the human moment a name because I believe that it has started to disappear from modern life—and I sense that we all may be about to discover the destructive power of its absence."[10]

This concept of keeping the human moment alive and well within an organization is a vital part of the re-visioning process. Leaders must build into their lives and into the fabric of their organizations ways to refresh the relationships that provide life and vibrancy. This is not always easy, because human contact takes energy and focus and thus can tax one's already overextended life. It may be easier to send a colleague an e-mail, but that does not mean it's better.

I will often walk down the hall or stop by an office on the other side of campus to check in or follow up on some item of business. The rewards are always worth the time. I could have received the information I needed via e-mail, but I could not have made the same type of connection that comes from a personal visit, particularly from the president. Those moments breathe fresh breath into relationships. Hallowell elaborates:

> The positive effects of a human moment can last long after the people involved have said goodbye and walked away. People begin to think in new and creative ways; mental activity is stimulated. But like exercise, which also has enduring effects, the benefits of a human moment do not last indefinitely. You must engage in human moments on a regular basis for them to have a meaningful impact on your life.[11]

What happens when this level of human interaction is absent? Hallowell suggests that it is replaced by worry, often toxic worry. The vacuum gets filled with a high level of anxiety. With this often comes a series of little misunderstandings, such as when an e-mail message is misconstrued or a voice mail message strikes the wrong tone. These types of things can create a negative culture.

To counter this, the strategic use of human interaction can reduce the confusion and ambiguity of electronic communications.

Not long ago my wife and I were with some family friends and their children. We were trying to connect with another family to arrange an evening meal. After a variety of texts and e-mails, which yielded no response, one of the boys in our group said to himself—but just loud enough for all of us to hear—"Why don't you people just *call* them?" A good question.

Technology has created a magnificent new world, bursting with opportunity. It has opened up a global, knowledge-based economy and unchained people from their desks. We are all in its debt—and we are never going back. But we cannot afford to move forward successfully without preserving the human moment. . . . The human moment provides the zest and color in the painting of our daily lives; it restores us, strengthens us, and makes us whole.[12]

SECTION 3
THE LOOK AHEAD

9
RE
TICULATE

The secret of getting ahead is getting started. The secret to getting started is breaking your complex, overwhelming tasks into small manageable tasks and then starting on the first one.
—Mark Twain

Everything is affected by and is part of everything else, changing constantly from one state to another. The rain becomes the river; the river surrenders to the sea and the cycle begins over again. Nothing is ever lost. The melody changes—the dance goes on.
—Connie Harrison

First comes thought; then organization of that thought into ideas and plans; then transformation of those plans into reality. The beginning, as you will observe, is in your imagination.
—Napoleon Hill

To *reticulate* is "to form a net or a network." As a verb it means to form or assume a certain shape, such as the redesign of a manufacturing process planned so that the parts fit together in a more cohesive manner. It can mean to change, to become different in pattern or form. I once saw a silver necklace that was in the form of beautiful sleek netting. It had been reticulated to resemble a light gossamer shape.

The term can also mean to distribute through a network. As an adjective, the term means to create something that resembles a network or formal system.

Transforming an organization requires a new vision, coupled with new ways of thinking about strategy, structure, and people. "While some entrepreneurs can start with a clean slate, transformational leaders must begin with what is already in place. They are like architects who redesign outmoded factories for a new use."[1] This image of a leader as an architect is "right on" if an organization is to be re-visioned. Many of the old patterns and systems will have to give way to new designs.

There are moments in the life of most organizations when the various ways the organization functions need to be redesigned for added efficiency. This can be an important step in the re-visioning process. Yet it can often be accompanied by a certain drama, which, if handled correctly, can be a positive force rather than a source of organizational anxiety.

These dramas generally play out in three acts. In the first act the leader takes center stage as he or she sets forth the need for change and begins to encounter the inevitable and necessary questions and challenges to the prospect that things will have to be different going forward. This realization brings about the natural struggle between the forces of stability ("This is the way we have always done it") and the external as well as internal forces of change. The changing realities that impact an organization's viability going forward are often subtle enough, particularly to the average employee, that they are not immediately recognized. Like the frog in the proverbial beaker of water that is getting hotter little by little, organizations can fail to realize the need for change until it is too late.

The American automobile industry is a classic example. Little by little, foreign competition began to wear away the competitive advantage of "the big three." Though in some cases senior leadership recognized the danger, it was not until bankruptcy set in that the alarm bells went off for the average Detroit worker. By then, however, it was too late for many who continued to protest the needed changes even as their factories were boarded up and their jobs disappeared.

The stress of this tug-of-war between what is and what should be is experienced primarily by middle managers who have senior leaders pointing them in one direction and coworkers who are generally satisfied with the way things are and see no need to change. The feelings of many throughout an organization in the early stages of renewal are often expressed verbally or nonverbally as a desire for the ways things used to be. *Why do we keep changing things? We've been doing just fine.*

The senior leadership team must provide a steady stream of encouragement and key information to managers and their people to keep the possibility and need for change clearly in view. Information and plenty of time for employees to process the proposed changes help to counter the natural anxiety about change. Solid, timely information also helps an organization withstand an often pervasive unawareness or even denial of a changing reality, which left unmet could bring serious negative implications.

Leaders must be able to balance the need for change with the need for stability. They must recognize and acknowledge the struggle between fear and hope on the part of many who have been with the organization for a long time. These individuals may recognize a need for change but remain fearful of what that will mean, particularly for them. Hope and optimism are the antidotes. This "hope" factor transcends the level of wishing and is certainly more than crossing one's fingers and saying, "I hope this works." The hope that sustains and energizes the renewal process is a settled hope, rooted not in wishes and daydreams but in solid planning and research.

Thus, leaders involved in renewal must create a fresh vision that at least most employees will view as desirable. "Leaders must pull the organization into the future by creating a positive view of what the organization can become and simultaneously provide emotional support for individuals during the transition process."[2]

Next comes the second act. In these next few scenes the leader is fully engaged in shaping a new set of expectations and seeking to project a preferred future for the organization and all its various stakeholders. This is a process—not a pronouncement. Organizations will need some time to adjust. One need not resist periods of pausing during the implementation phase to allow people to adjust to the changing environment. Like a deep-sea diver who cannot withstand a sudden ascent, organizations and employees will benefit from certain neutral or "time-out" periods. Often when Jill and I return from an extended trip, we talk about the need for our spirits to catch up with us. Organizations need such moments as well so that by the end of this act there is a tentative yet positive and energized air of expectancy.

In the third and final act of the drama, the leader seeks to stabilize and institutionalize the results of the re-visioning so that gains made will survive his or her tenure. This is far from automatic. In fact, one of the often unexpected issues to deal with is frustration that accompanies the almost inevitable moments of failure that may occur as new methods and procedures are implemented. Adequate training and support must be provided.

Reticulation is a key element in this stage, for it puts into place new systems and processes that not only preserve the accomplishments of the past but also continually foster a corporate culture of innovation and flexibility. Revitalization is empty until the new vision becomes reality. The whole process will evaporate during the heat of the day if the new way of thinking does not make its way into day-to-day practice. New realities, expectations, actions, and practices must be shared throughout the organization if change is to become institutionalized.

The reticulation process, which flows from a new or renewed vision for the organization, will touch on three basic areas if that vision is to become reality. The first is the basic design of how an organization functions. People, money, technical resources, and basic operating systems must be arranged to help minimize the impact of both external and internal changes in business environmental that undermine the organization's productivity and viability while maximizing the opportunities that may be embedded within those same changes.

There was a time, several years into my presidency, when the prospects and untapped potential of our graduate and non-traditional degree programs seemed to call out for a new organizational structure that would allow these programs to reach their full potential. To re-vision this part of our work meant a change in university structure from top to bottom. I envisioned a new position—Vice President for Graduate and Continuing Studies—along with the renaming and reorganization of that division of our work, which would provide more autonomy and flexibility and a decentralization of certain departments on campus that were designed to serve the traditional eighteen- to twenty-two-year-old student rather than the working adult learner.

While nearly everyone I talked with affirmed the need for the graduate school to expand, not everyone wanted to accommodate the changes that would be necessary. First, for decades the senior leadership team of the university—known as the administrative team—consisted of the president and four vice presidents in the respective areas of academics, business and finance, student development, and institutional advancement. The change I envisioned would change that structure by adding a fifth vice president. At different points in the process of discussing this, I encountered both a lack of enthusiasm on the part of some and a firm vocal objection from one vice president.

Yet I felt strongly that this important area needed focused, senior leadership and a full integration into the life of the university, which would happen only with an expansion of the senior leadership team. Given sufficient time to process the idea, seasoned with a firm commitment on my part, the adjustment was made. The other members of the administrative team embraced the new structure and were particularly helpful in welcoming and integrating the newly appointed additional vice president into the group.

In the years following, other vital functions such as transcript evaluations, student financial aid, student accounts, marketing, information technology, and so on have been decentralized to a degree to enable the graduate school to function with an appropriate level of autonomy and speed. Other issues related to this new structure regarding lines of authority and decision-making processes have also had to be clarified and improved.

One important part of this reticulation was the continual campus-wide dialogue about mission and values. Once there was clear agreement on those core issues and a level of trust in the fact that others also shared those commitments, it became easier to let go of some long-held procedures that had often been held onto tightly as a way of ensuring clarity of mission.

A clarification at this point might be helpful: it is important to note the distinction between a values conflict and a difference of opinion. All organizations can benefit from open and honest debate and differences of opinion. The very nature of higher education certainly rests in part on the process of challenging prevailing opinions. The goal in re-visioning should not be to expect or demand that everyone be of one mind—it is more a matter of everyone being of one *heart.*

Effective leaders help the organization's members reframe the way in which they think about their common problems. To do this, leaders must be aware of some basic reasons people can be resistant to change and then develop a strategy to address these issues. For example, one common and often subconscious threat lies in the tension that develops between the old guard and the new guard. When change begins, it can affect how individuals and groups of individuals—departments, for example—interface with others. Old patterns and alliances often have to give way to new groupings. This is an unsettling process for many.

Another factor that can result in active or passive resistance to change is the recognition that resources will need to be realigned. Often the message from senior leadership is that the organization must find ways to be more productive and innovative with a smaller head count and fewer discretionary dollars. These "zero sum" decisions are politically challenging and difficult to implement.

A third item that often results in resistance to change is the implication that change means some level of indictment of past decisions. While such an implication need not be true for every anticipated change, the perception still may have some level of acceptance. It is naturally difficult for people to change when they have not participated in the creation of the process or procedures that are now being changed.

In addition, some proposed changes can be perceived as threatening to an individual's future and career opportunities. Any of these factors can result in inaction or even vocal and active resistance. Leaders who seek to renew their organizations will need to be proactive and positive in responding to these issues.

Leaders who initiate change know that it is not unusual for the most challenging aspects of re-visioning to lie in the implementation and especially in the creation of a framework and environment of confidence and anticipation. It is here where the tensions between the organizational goals and objectives and the individual aspirations and anxieties come into play.

Some writers and theorists use the metaphor of a "strategic rope" to illustrate this point. From a distance, a rope may appear as a single, solid strand. It is, however, many strands joined to form a much stronger and more flexible entity than any of the strands alone could be. The strength of the rope depends not only on the strength of the individual strands but also on their connection. Just as a rope can unravel, an organization can come apart if its people and processes begin to work at cross purposes.

The task of a transformational leader seeking to provide leadership across a long period of time is to have the ability to reweave the rope as necessary by adding new strands. The new strands then become fully interwoven with the older, and by repairing existing strands—systems and relationships and employee skills— as needed. Often employees can catch a second wind if they are involved in and exposed to the process of re-vision and planning for the future.

Leaders who last learn how people deal with change, both generally and in ways that may be specifically germane to one's given organization. Overcoming resistance by individuals who have become acclimated to the old ways is much more complicated than simply issuing a directive. People need and deserve a way to work through the psychological challenges of giving up the known and comfortable ways in which they have worked to transition to a new normal. Employees and organizations must work through the weight of habit and inertia. These are natural forces, and thus it is unnatural to expect those issues not to be in play. Individuals also need some time and support to process the fear of the unknown and/or loss of organizational and workplace predictability.

One of the things we have done at the university is to send our key employees, not just senior leaders, to visit schools, organizations, and businesses that already have in place the changes we are proposing. From examining a different floor-waxing system to reviewing a state-of-the-art academic support lab and organization to kicking the tires on a different mower to a professional consultation with a peer institution concerning their success at student retention—there is genuine value in providing opportunities for frontline employees to discover for themselves the changes you may wish to implement.

Another key to the people side of re-visioning is to be able to identify those who are on board and those who will need more time before becoming fully engaged in the new reality. When the personal computer wave first hit higher education, some jumped in with joy and anticipation, while a significant number of others ran for the hills. At Olivet, as we began the monumental job of bringing the entire university into line with the new technology, we quickly discovered that it was a hard thing to require of people who were not yet ready.

What worked best for us was to identify those individuals and/ or departments that were eager to make the transition to a fully computer-integrated workplace and/or learning environment, then resource those individuals to begin the process. At first, training was offered and encouraged but not demanded. Later everyone would need to be trained, but not at first. We also held brainstorming sessions with those who already could see the benefits of computerization for their work. We sent those individuals to conferences and connected them with software companies and computer specialists.

As soon as a department was ready, we provided the hardware. Little by little, offices began to fill with computers, and there were computer labs showing up here and there throughout the academic buildings. Soon others who had and perhaps still were resistant began to take notice. *Why did they get a computer lab and not us?* was the implied question. The administration responded by offering the same level of training, encouragement, and support to the second wave of implementers. Before long the new reality seemed much less threatening and was embraced by all.

An important aspect of leadership during these periods of change is for there to be consistent, positive reminders of why the changes are taking place. To do this, leaders need a clear transitional agenda list of those things that must be done for re-visioning to take hold at an implementation level. There also should be a public acknowledgment that there are no easy answers and that the problems for some, which are a direct result of the changes being made, are indeed legitimate challenges. Leaders cannot afford to minimize the real stress of change. However, that stress need not—in fact must not—paralyze the progress. Often individuals who are struggling with change just want to be sure others recognize and express at least some measure of empathy and support.

Also, it is helpful for leaders not to beat the drum too loudly. Often those who are leading change have a tendency to oversell the concept. This can create a climate of over-expectation and/or a psychological fatigue from the constant talk of change.

Another key leadership skill for effectiveness over time is the ability to distinguish between an event and a trend. Some challenges and some opportunities are singular events that may call for one's momentary attention but do not represent transformational trends. I have observed a few individuals in leadership who seem to be constantly in a state of flux. They appear fearful that they will be caught off guard by some new development. As a prolonged pattern, this not only distorts the leader's focus but also creates a sustained unsettledness throughout the organization.

There is a necessary tension at this point, for leaders do need to be weather forecasters, noting changes in the seasons. This is both an art and a science. I remember quite clearly when I first heard of the Internet and its World Wide Web. That moment came during my second year as president, and it became a catalyst for reorganizing our approach to communication, learning, and campus life.

When our director of computer services finished his administrative briefing about this new phenomenon, I was stunned. Immediately I could see the enormous challenges we would face in trying to move our campus into this digital realm. I knew we had no choice but to respond comprehensively and quickly. We needed to adjust rapidly to this new reality.

I MET A MAN

I had a fitting with a tailor not long ago. The unusual thing about it was that it happened in an aisle at a local grocery store. Following work one afternoon, I stopped by the store to pick up a handful of items. As I started down a long aisle, I saw a man at the far end whom I didn't know but knew I *should* know. He saw me and waved. I waved back and quickly began sorting through my mental contact list, hoping I could pull a name or some association that would help me with what was surely going to be an inevitable conversation.

Soon we were standing face to face in the middle of the aisle near the cereal. I said, "Hello—I haven't seen you for a while."

"Yes, it *has* been a long time," he replied.

"How are you?" I asked.

"Well, not too good," was his response. "You know that Ruthie passed away, and I moved to Chicago with my daughter and her family. It's very nice, but not the same. I'm just back in town for a few days to visit my sister Colleen."

With that sentence, I had it. He had given me just enough information I could use to begin to pull together a distant set of memories. As I continued to search for a name, he said, "You look good, and the school just keeps getting better."

Then, with both hands, he gently adjusted the shoulders of my suit and glanced at the sleeves. With those gestures it all came back to me. For many years this kind man had owned a fine men's clothing store in the community. I first met him during my student days and had continued to shop there when I returned as a faculty member and during the first few years I was president until his shop closed. Although he had not worked as a tailor for many years, it was still in his nature to "check the fit."

Leaders are tailors as well. They look, measure, and evaluate with a constant eye to right-sizing. Just as an individual's clothing must be adjusted over time in light of changing waistlines or prevailing styles, organizations need a "fitting" from time to time as well.

IT'S WHAT'S INSIDE THAT COUNTS

I am very particular about time—being on time, starting on time, and ending on time. I suppose my office staff and the administrators with whom I work most closely would tell you the word is not *particular* but rather *compulsive* about time. Okay, maybe I am just a little. In fact, I wrote a doctoral dissertation on the subject of time management, so I suppose they have a point.

Because of my interest in time, I also have an interest in clocks and watches. A few years ago while strolling through an antique shop, I spotted what appeared to be a fine old watch. I recognized the name on the face and was surprised at the low price. I asked to see the watch and was told that it was quite rare, but because the market for such a watch was so limited, the price had been reduced. I bought the watch.

A few days later I was surprised and disappointed when the watch stopped running. I took it to a local jeweler and learned that the inner workings of the watch were not from the fine watch company that had made the case. The inner workings had been replaced by a very poor mechanism that could not be repaired and thus would never keep good time.

This experience reminded me just how important all the inner workings of a watch really are. Appearance doesn't matter much if the watch doesn't run with precision and consistency. It's what's *inside* that counts; it's what is rarely seen that determines true quality and dependability.

The same is true for a university. Behind the scenes every day are a myriad of movements combining to create the university that is seen and experienced in public. To highlight this, several years ago a group of Olivet students spent the day documenting "A Day in the Life of Olivet." They took hundreds of photographs of the myriad of campus activities throughout the day.

These pictures represent a photographic diary—a journal—a series of snapshots of the many people who made the school "tick." The work of any organization is always a team effort—men and women who embody and express the mission of the organization on a daily basis.

PICK A NUMBER—ANY NUMBER

Pick a number—any number. Got it? Okay.

Did you pick a number larger than one million? Probably not. People don't usually think in terms of millions. Yet the choosing of a number can be very significant. Sometimes the numbers we choose, when we can choose any number, matter.

About ten years ago two graduate students at Stanford University picked a number. The number they chose was the number 1 followed by one hundred zeros. Do you know what that number is called? It is known as a "googol." That is how much information these two students dreamed of processing with a new Internet search engine.

To keep the dream in front of them, they named their company "Google." And now, just a few years later, there are tens of millions of searches through Google every day, accessing billions of pages of information in nearly one hundred languages. And the term "googling" has become synonymous with web-surfing.

Google has become a huge company and a dominant part of our culture. It all began with the number those two Stanford students chose. Their number, 1 followed by one hundred zeros, wasn't just a number. It was a dream; and those students decided to dream big.

Leaders and key managers must be men and women with the capacity to dream big as well. Years ago when I was in college, one of the books we read as students was J. B. Phillips' book *Your God Is Too Small.* The first half of the book is given to deconstructing many of the distorted images of God that keep people from truly seeing and coming to faith in Him. In the second half of the book, Dr. Phillips reconstructs a logical framework for understanding a truer vision of God. With the precision of a surgeon and the heart of a pastor, Phillips spoke spiritual truth to a generation—my generation—just starting to experience the collapse of the modern era.

In the years since his book was first published, much has changed; yet from time to time we are still prone to worship a God who is much too small. Pick a number—any number.

EASY EDDIE

For many years the gangster Al Capone controlled much of the city of Chicago. He was notorious for a crime wave across the Windy City involving everything from bootlegged booze and prostitution to murder. Among his closest associates was an attorney, "Easy Eddie." He was Capone's lawyer for a good reason: his skill at legal maneuvering kept Al out of jail for many years. To show his appreciation, Capone paid Easy Eddie very well. Not only was the money big, but Eddie also got special dividends. For instance, he and his family occupied a fenced-in mansion with live-in help and all the conveniences of the day. The estate was so large that it filled an entire Chicago city block.

Eddie lived the high life of the Chicago mob and gave little consideration to the atrocities that went on around him. Eddie did have one soft spot, however. He had a son whom he loved dearly. Eddie saw to it that his young son had clothes, cars, and a good education. Nothing was withheld. Price was no object. And despite his involvement with organized crime, Eddie even tried to teach his boy right from wrong.

Eddie wanted his son to be a better man than he was. Yet with all the wealth and influence, there were two things he couldn't give his son—he could not pass on a good name or a good example.

One day Easy Eddie reached a difficult decision. He wanted to rectify wrongs he had done. He decided he would go to the authorities and tell the truth about Al Capone, clean up his tarnished name, and offer his son some semblance of integrity. He would have to testify against organized crime, and he knew that the cost would be great.

He testified, and within the year Easy Eddie's life ended in a blaze of gunfire on a lonely Chicago street. But in his eyes he had given his son the greatest gift he had to offer—at the greatest price he could ever pay. Police removed from his pockets a rosary, a crucifix, a religious medallion, and a poem clipped from a magazine. The poem read—

> *The clock of life is wound but once,*
> *And no man has the power*
> *To tell just when the hands will stop*
> *At late or early hour.*
> *Now is the only time you own.*
> *Live, love, toil with a will.*
> *Place no faith in time.*
> *For the clock may soon be still.*[3]

EASY EDDIE: A FOLLOW-UP STORY

World War II produced many heroes. One such hero was Lieutenant Commander Butch O'Hare, a fighter pilot assigned to the aircraft carrier *Lexington* in the South Pacific. One day his entire squadron was sent on a mission. After he was airborne, he looked at his fuel gage and realized that someone had forgotten to top off his fuel tank. He would not have enough fuel to complete his mission and get back to his ship. His flight leader told him to return to the carrier. Reluctantly, he dropped out of formation and headed back to the fleet.

As he was returning to the mother ship, he saw something that turned his blood cold: a squadron of Japanese aircraft speeding its way toward the American fleet. The American fighters were gone on a mission, and the fleet was all but defenseless. He couldn't reach his squadron on the radio to bring them back in time to save the fleet. Nor could he warn the fleet of the approaching danger.

There was only one thing to do. He must somehow divert the enemy from the fleet. Laying aside all thoughts of personal safety, he dove into the formation of Japanese planes. Wing-mounted fifty-calibers blazed as he charged in, attacking one surprised enemy plane and then another. Butch maneuvered in and out of the now-broken formation and fired at as many planes as possible until all his ammunition was finally spent. Undaunted, he continued the assault. He dove at the planes, trying to clip a wing or tail in hopes of damaging as many enemy planes as possible and rendering them unfit to fly.

Finally, the exasperated Japanese squadron took off in another direction. Deeply relieved, Butch O'Hare and his tattered fighter limped back to the carrier. Upon arrival, he reported in and related the event surrounding his return. The film from the gun-camera mounted on his plane told the tale. It showed the extent of Butch's daring attempt to protect his fleet. He had, in fact, destroyed five enemy aircraft.

This took place on February 20, 1942, and for that action Butch O'Hare became the Navy's first Ace of World War II and the first naval aviator to win the Congressional Medal of Honor. A year later Butch was killed in aerial combat at the age of twenty-nine. His hometown would not allow the memory of this WW II hero to fade, and today O'Hare Airport in Chicago is named in tribute to the courage of this great man.

Oh, by the way—Butch O'Hare was "Easy Eddie's" son. The next time you find yourself at O'Hare, give some thought to visiting Butch's memorial displaying his statue and his Medal of Honor.[4]

The life that might have been for the son of "Easy Eddie" was supplanted by a new life, one of honor and sacrifice. Just as individuals can change, so can organizations, enabling them to exchange what *would* be for what *could* be with a new vision.

10

RE
ARTICULATE

When I face the desolate impossibility of writing 500 pages,
a sick sense of failure falls on me, and I know I can never do it.
Then gradually, I write one page and then another. One day's work
is all that I can permit myself to contemplate.
—John Steinbeck

Some stories don't have a clear beginning, middle and end. Life is about not
knowing, having to change, taking the moment and making the best of it,
without knowing what's going to happen next.
—Gilda Radner

Don't wait for something big to occur. Start where you are, with what
you have, and that will always lead you into something greater.
—Mary Manin Morrissey

One December Jill and I attended the all-school Christmas party
on campus and later stopped by Brian and Lynda Allen's house
for a few minutes. Brian and Lynda both work at the university.
While we were there, their son, Kyle—who was a student at the
university—also dropped by with some of his friends. Jill and I
greeted the students as they made their way to the basement—by
way of the kitchen.

When we got home later that night, I said to Jill, "I'm going to stay downstairs to study for a little bit." She went on upstairs to get ready for bed. About a half hour later, just as I was wrapping up my reading, I got a text message on my cell phone from Jill. It said, "How ya' doin', Tiger?"

I hit "reply" and typed, "I'll be right up."

As I walked into the bedroom, I said, "Hey, I got your message."

She said, "What message?"

"Your text message."

"I didn't send you a message," she replied. "In fact, a few minutes ago I realized that I must have left my phone at Brian and Lynda's."

Then it hit me. The message on my phone, "How ya doin', Tiger?" was really from those students pretending to be Jill, and I had replied, "I'll be right up." In a few moments I got another message. This time it was a picture of those kids smiling and waving to me from in front of the Allens' Christmas tree, as if to say, "Gotcha!"

I loved the creativity and humor embedded in that experience; but I also have come to see that moment as instructive. It illustrates the value and vulnerability of our formal and informal communications. Leaders who remain effective over long periods of time are able to measure and ensure the effectiveness of their communications regarding an organizations values, vision, and processes. One cannot assume that all communications are reaching the intended audience or understood fully. Therefore, effective leaders need to pay close attention to the frequency, form, content, and feedback related to internal and external messaging. This is particularly true once change is underway. A constant re-articulation must precede, accompany, and follow institutional change.

THE SPEECH

Part of a leader's role is to be the institutional storyteller—the one above all others who provides and keeps a unifying narrative alive. In *Reinventing Leadership: Strategies to Empower the Organization*, the authors make a special point of emphasizing the vital role of personal communication for leaders, noting that one of the reasons people are drawn to a leader is that he or she makes them feel significant and included in important ways. "Leaders communicate their vision to those around them in ways that emotionally enroll others to turn this vision into reality."[1]

In my work, one aspect of this has come to be known as "the speech." I give this same talk each summer to freshman at their orientation sessions, each fall to new faculty orientations, and once a quarter at new employee luncheons. It is a speech in which I tell the story of the founding of the university and give an overview of its history and development.

One year as we were preparing for one of the freshman orientation dinners, a group of upperclassmen who were working as ambassadors with the Admissions Department gathered around me to talk. In the course of the conversation one young man asked, "Dr. Bowling, are you going to give 'the speech'?" Without answering, I just began: "Olivet Nazarene University began as an idea—a big idea in the minds and hearts of a handful of eastern Illinois families at the beginning of the last century. . . ." In a flash the students were retelling the story with me.

"I like it when you talk about the fire that destroyed the old campus," one said.

"The best part," a young lady suggested, "is when you say, 'In one hand he had a college without a campus and in the other a campus without a college.'"

These students knew the story, not just because they had heard it several times but because it had become *their* story. They owned the Olivet story as part of their personal experience, and it provided a way of understanding their day-to-day interactions on campus. In the process of re-visioning, leaders must put "the story" of their organizations into words and images. Leaders need to paint a mental picture that will address not just what has been but, more important, what *will* be.

ADVERTISING SLOGANS

Advertisers know a good slogan when they see it. Along with being catchy and memorable, a slogan must also convey something important about the product it represents. The professional journal *Advertising Age* ranked the following among the top slogans used in the last several years:

1. You deserve a break today (McDonalds).
2. Just do it (Nike).
3. The pause that refreshes (Coca-Cola)
4. Where's the beef? (Wendy's)
5. We try harder (Avis).
6. Good to the last drop (Maxwell House)
7. The breakfast of champions (Wheaties)
8. The milk chocolate melts in your mouth, not in your hand (M&Ms).
9. When it rains it pours (Morton Salt).
10. Tastes great, less filling (Miller Lite).[2]

After years of having such phrases drummed into our ears, who could forget them? And more important, who among us has not been influenced by those messages? However, to me the most striking thing about the list is that most of those phrases are no longer used. Coke no longer uses "The pause that refreshes," and McDonalds no longer uses "You deserve a break today."

Slogans, as good as they are, enjoy only a limited shelf-life. When first used, they strike the hearer as fresh, but with time and repetition their effectiveness begins wearing off. Eventually the phrases become so familiar that they no longer impact the hearer as they once did.

We have a set of slogans that have been used for Olivet across the years. Presently we're using the phrase "We believe . . . you belong." Just before that, we used "We believe higher education should have a higher purpose." That is one of my favorites—in fact (don't tell our marketing department), I still use it.

Yet, knowing that one day these slogans for Olivet will also be replaced, it is important for us to have a clear sense of identity that resides at a deeper level than a slogan. Therefore, in addition to the slogans, we also have a motto, and the motto of the university has not changed over the years: "An education with a Christian purpose."

What is the difference between a motto and slogan? Slogans come and go; mottos come to stay. Why is that? Mottos stay because they flow directly from mission rather than marketing. The mission statement of Olivet is this:

> Olivet Nazarene University, a denominational university in the Wesleyan tradition, exists to provide a liberal arts "education with a Christian purpose." Our mission is to provide high quality academic instruction for the purpose of personal development, career and professional readiness, and the preparation of individuals for lives of service to God and humanity.

For Olivet Nazarene University to be all it should be, each member of the faculty and staff must bear the marks of the university. The marks of the university need to become part of each individual's personal DNA.

Philip Eaton, the president of Seattle Pacific University for many years, makes a compelling case for organizations to link their stories with a larger overarching narrative. He writes, "The philosophical, cultural and educational orthodoxy of our day says there is no big map, no overarching story, no drama into which we are swept."[3]

He goes on to describe the world that exists with no unifying story, suggesting in the words of Chaim Potok that "We live in a world of colliding maps."[4] In such an environment, the need to articulate the role and significance of one's organization is a vital step. We must find ways for our past and present to overlap in ways that set the stage for the future.

With the administrative team fully committed, our Vice President for Academic Affairs and I led the charge. Through group meetings, an on-line survey, and other feedback mechanisms, the following list of core values was developed. This document became a formal articulation of the everyday values, which are woven into the life of the university. By providing a campus-wide process to develop and vet this document, the entire university community became involved in what turned out to be a shared articulation.

These value statements were "field tested" by asking the directors and department heads to meet with their teams to view the proposed list, make any suggestions they might have as to the nature and wording of the values, and then, most important, discuss how their work might be different in the light of these values. This step in the process proved to be invaluable as the entire faculty and staff were engaged in thinking and talking about what values most appropriately define the university—both actually and aspirationally.

The final document is as follows:

Our Values
OLIVET NAZARENE UNIVERSITY
Bourbonnais, Illinois

Preamble

The value statements of Olivet Nazarene University flow from and provide context and reinforcement for the mission of the University. The mission statement of the University expresses the why of its existence. The value statements express how that mission is experienced as it is lived out among the various constituents and dimensions of university life. The mission statement is as follows:

Olivet Nazarene University, a denominational university in the Wesleyan tradition, exists to provide a liberal arts "Education with a Christian Purpose." Our mission is to provide high quality academic instruction for the purpose of personal development, career and professional readiness, and the preparation of individuals for lives of service to God and humanity.

This mission drives the University in an educational and theological direction. It provides a touchstone by which its existence is measured.

Value Statements

In pursuing our mission, Olivet Nazarene University is guided by a shared set of values, which we consider central to our identity. We value:

Christ-Centeredness: Christ transforms people and the University.

The Olivet story is a Kingdom story. Christ is always at work, reconciling humankind to God and the University to His purpose. We therefore remain optimistic that He is at work in our instruction, scholarship, discipleship, and activities, and He enables us to live a holy life.

Community: Sharing life is sacred.

Our work is a shared work. We are made one by the work of the Holy Spirit. His work is not confined to religious initiatives, but transforms our community as He lives within us, guiding us in all things, whether on ground or online, in residence halls or extension sites, in offices or lecture halls, in professional or personal relationships. In community, we express His grace to each another.

Stewardship: God expects a return on His provision.

Since God's resources are abundant, scarcity is unfamiliar to Him. He supplies everything needed to accomplish His purpose. We remain joyfully accountable to maximize what He entrusts to us—time, talent, treasure, and opportunity—and wisely allocate His resources in our care. "To whom much is given, much is required."

Innovation: We respond quickly to need.

God is at work in the world, ever redeeming people through boundless and creative works of the Holy Spirit. We seek a proactive, creative role in impacting people and culture for His sake. We, therefore, seize opportunity, exercise responsible ambition, and delight in His expansive work through us.

Distinction: We make extraordinary impact.

One demonstration of Christlikeness is extraordinary servanthood: going the extra mile and abounding in love. We invite, encourage, and assist our faculty and staff to become experts, accrue recognized credentials, and provide the highest levels of service and professionalism. By this we bring honor to God and secure a place of documented quality among the nation's best Christian universities.

Heritage: A legacy lives in heart and practice.

Olivet's history is punctuated by God's providence and provision. We drink from wells we did not dig and eat from vines we did not plant. The vision and confidence of those who came before reside in us, because we believe the original mission is still relevant, ennobling, and necessary. Our traditions honor and exercise that legacy, refresh our identity as a faithful and favored people, fuel excellence and holiness for our time, and inspire optimism for a future illuminated by the Light of God.

WHERE ARE MY GLASSES?

As I was getting ready to leave the house one morning to go to a breakfast meeting and then to the office, I realized I couldn't find my glasses. Finally I had to retrieve an old pair from a drawer and wear them throughout the day. I was able to function all right, but everything was slightly out of focus.

That experience reminded me in a personal way of two very important things: (1) Each person sees the world through a unique set of lenses, and (2) the lens through which one views the world makes all of the difference. To illustrate this, at one of our regular faculty and staff gatherings, I asked those in the group who were wearing glasses to hand their eyewear to the person seated to their right and for that person to put on those glasses. The room filled with laughter as people tried to look at the world through various lenses.

What is the difference between a microscope and a telescope? The lens. The shape and contour of the lens determines what one sees. Change the lens, and you change your understanding of reality. A telescope sees out to the far reaches of the sky. In contrast, a microscope brings the smallest items into view.

Each leader and the individuals he or she works with have a worldview. There are times when people are navigating situations without the proper lenses necessary to interpret what they see, or worse, they go through life wearing someone else's glasses so that what they see is distorted. Often progress within a company or working group can be improved simply by coordinating and communicating clearly how each member sees a given situation.

If you have ever watched a three-dimensional film, you know that what happens on the screen makes sense only when it is viewed through the special 3D glasses. If you take the glasses off for a moment, the film suddenly loses its focus, and things become distorted. In much the same way, the world around us makes sense and stays in focus only when we view it through a proper set of lenses.

GOING ON VACATION

When I was a boy, my family took annual vacations. Nothing elaborate—usually we drove our station wagon to a neighboring state, stayed a few nights in a motel, and visited some place of interest such as Abe Lincoln's house or the Wisconsin Dells. On our travels my father often bought copies of various local newspapers.

He took time in the evening to scan each paper from a technical point of view. He was a newspaper publisher, so he was interested in the type style, the weight of the paper, and the number of column inches devoted to advertising. My mother, on the other hand, read the local news, looked at the ads, and often tore out a story or a recipe. My older brother went for the sports section, and I grabbed the comics.

Same family. Same newspaper. Different interests.

This concept underscores the need for leaders to know their strengths and weaknesses. To re-vision an organization, there must be careful analysis of organizational structure and culture. There must also be a process of self-assessment on the part of key leaders. This process must include a look at one's feelings, values, and personality strengths and weaknesses and must go beyond a single leader. It is not possible for a single leader, working alone, to transform a large, complex organization. Leaders by definition must enlist followers who share the leader's sense of urgency about the need for change and who join in framing the problem.

Dr. Martin Luther King created an enormously inspiring vision in his famous "I Have a Dream" address at the Washington Monument. In that speech he painted a picture of a United States that would be a better place. He talked about the little children, white and black, playing and holding hands in the rural towns in Alabama; blacks and whites working together in urban centers. That vision had a motivational pull. It created a positive image that people could strive for.[5]

This underscores the importance of fostering a cohesive group of leaders who embrace a common vision and culture. Effective leaders assess an organization's strengths and weaknesses and measure those against the broad environmental opportunities. They also articulate the challenges and opportunities that inspire employees to meet those challenges.

HALLMARK HALL OF FAME

In the past few years I have had the opportunity to get acquainted with Brad Moore, president of Hallmark Hall of Fame Productions. It is a subsidiary of Hallmark Cards, Inc., of Kansas City. Brad is responsible for all aspects of *Hallmark Hall of Fame,* considered by many as the most honored series in United States television history.

Moore has led the *Hallmark Hall of Fame* for twenty-nine years, nearly half of its sixty-one-year existence. Under his leadership the series has produced over one hundred feature-length movies and received thirty-one Emmy awards (five for "Best Picture") plus seven Golden Globe awards and numerous other honors. Those films include the single most honored program in United States television history and the four movies with the largest audiences on any U.S. television network over the past twenty years.

Hallmark Cards, Inc., was founded in 1910 and today is the world's leading producer of greeting cards and related products. With over four billion dollars in annual revenue, Hallmark is a diversified international company with subsidiary or licensee/distributor businesses in more than one hundred countries and thirty languages. Its leading retail brands include Hallmark, DaySpring, Shoebox Greetings, and Crayola.

While leading the *Hallmark Hall of Fame,* Moore has also served in a variety of other responsibilities at Hallmark. He is currently a director of Crown Media Holdings, which operates the Hallmark Channel. He was president of Hallmark Publishing for two years. He directed all Hallmark advertising and promotion activities in the United States for fifteen years. For seven years he directed advertising activities for Hallmark subsidiaries in Europe, Asia, and Australia/New Zealand. Before joining Hallmark, Moore spent ten years at Procter & Gamble, where he held the positions of brand manager and associate advertising manager.

Outside of Hallmark, Moore serves as chairman of the board of trustees of a university and past chair and current member of the board of a publishing company. He is also a member of the Production Executives Peer Group of the Academy of Television Arts & Sciences and a past director of both the Association of National Advertisers and Kansas City public television station KCPT.

In his leisure time he enjoys entertaining his five grandchildren, playing golf, and riding his 2003 Harley-Davidson "Screaming Eagle Deuce." In 2005 he and two friends rode five thousand miles from their driveways to the Arctic Circle via Canada and Alaska. In 2011 and 2012 he and friends rode their Harleys eleven thousand miles from the southern tip of South America back to their homes. They deemed the ride "Miles with a Mission," with supporters contributing "per mile" to raise nearly five hundred thousand dollars for university scholarships and for medical relief through Heart to Heart International.

Recently I asked Brad Moore a series of questions about what he has learned across the years and how his leadership has changed. His answers were insightful and demonstrated a grasp of what it takes to give steady and fresh leadership in an organization across a long span of time. Here are the questions and responses.

1. How have the nature and/or demands of your work changed across the years?

Brad pointed out that his work has changed in three fundamental ways across the years. First, there is far more complexity in the television competitive landscape than ever before. When he began his work at *Hallmark Hall of Fame* three national networks accounted for over ninety percent of all television viewing in the United States. The same networks now account for just over thirty percent. Little by little, and then all at once, it seemed, the entire media world was transformed to where there are now more than four hundred television channel choices in the United States and similar complexity around the world where the Hallmark movies are distributed via license agreements.

Another factor that helped Brad stay fresh as a senior leader was that he was able to take on a variety of added responsibilities over time while his *Hallmark Hall of Fame* responsibility remained constant. These other professional assignments put him in new situations with new people and new business challenges, each of which helped to constantly refresh his thinking and perspectives. Rather than letting his world shrink or narrow over time, he was able to keep pushing his own professional development.

Brad was able to stay connected with new trends and approaches to corporate leadership through his many opportunities to serve on various corporate and not-for-profit boards and to engage in other work assignments outside Hallmark. He intentionally put himself in situations where he would have to learn new lessons.

2. How have you been able to stay fully engaged and fresh in your work throughout your long span of service at Hallmark?

Moore stated, "The basic responsibilities of developing and producing movies are highly creative and stimulating. The subject matter of the stories, the characters, and the filming locations and requirements are constantly changing." And yet the quality of *Hallmark Hall of Fame* productions has stayed remarkably consistent across the years. Moore and the company's commitment to stay centered at a time when television and culture in general was undergoing huge changes is a lesson worth noting.

Hallmark Hall of Fame has been able to stay fresh through a combination of relevant and timely scripts that reflect a consistent set of core values, first rate production quality, top talent, and updates in style and format. These are all very visible to its millions of viewers. But equally important yet not visible to viewers are the substantial changes that have been made to the processes and business models used to develop and produce the movies and then to broadcast them in ways that reach the desired audience. The left brain/right brain work that is needed to lead both the creative side and the business side of the *Hallmark Hall of Fame* has kept Brad fresh and engaged— and has kept the series in the top tier of television productions.

Brad was also fortunate to find a line of professional work that fits his personality and temperament. He says, "Increased challenges generate energy in me. I love rising to the stimulation of solving problems and capitalizing on opportunities." This statement demonstrates a key element of long-term effective leadership—the work motivates and inspires the leader rather than depletes him or her. Leaders who last keep falling in love with their work year after year. It may be tough, demanding work, but it attracts their continued commitment and energy.

3. What have you learned about leadership during these years?

Among the lessons he learned on the job at Hallmark was the recognition that "leadership is not the same as managing—one must do both," he said. "Managing is often more comfortable, but certainly not as stimulating or fun." These statements reveal that Moore has been able to resist the pull to move his focus from the new to the normal. While maintaining business as usual is important for organizations if they are to ensure consistency of purpose and steady operations over time, it cannot be the sole focus of a senior leader. The core must remain steady, but the edges of the organization need to be flexible and responsive to market changes, challenges, and opportunities.

Race car driver Mario Andretti once observed that if everything is running smoothly, you aren't going fast enough. Energy comes from the growing edges of a company or organization. Brad is the type of executive who loves life on the edge. He said, "Leadership almost always involves change and always involves taking risks of some kind. Otherwise, it's simply not leadership." That is a terrific insight and definition of leadership: leadership without risk is not leadership—it is management, which is important but would not in itself move an organization forward or enable it to adapt to new challenges. Moore asserts, "Exerting leadership means you must be willing to be wrong and to admit it when you are."

Like great athletes, leaders never bat a thousand, don't always shoot below par, and aren't always first to cross the finish line. Yet they never stop getting back in the game. In the award-winning film *Chariots of Fire*, about the 1924 Olympics, one of the athletes loses an important race and in frustration declares, "If I can't win, I won't run." His friend counsels him, saying, "If you don't run, you can't win." To be in the race is to accept the risk of losing; but it also creates the possibility of winning.

As Brad Moore looked back across nearly three decades of senior leadership at Hallmark, he also noted that "Exerting leadership also means you must be willing to be criticized whether you deserve it or not. Leaders cannot please everyone." One of the most challenging aspects of leadership is to develop the ability both to listen to criticism and to ignore it at the same time. One most not become tone-deaf or dismissive of criticism—it is an important feedback loop. Yet leaders cannot become paralyzed by the risk of being criticized. Effective leaders learn to live on that fine line of listening and adjusting as necessary while at the same time continuing to lead.

Another aspect of Moore's successful leadership is his people skills. He is a top-flight people person. He has a genuine interest in others and values different points of view. He says, "Good leadership means working with and through others and giving or sharing credit for success. If it doesn't involve others, it's doing, not leading."

He puts his finger on a key point: one does not lead organizations per se—one leads *people*. That can be frustrating and trying from time to time, because people have issues and don't always meet expectations or agree on priorities or processes, but people are the organization.

In speaking of the need to find people who would fit the organization, Sharon Aby, a personnel recruiter for Apple, said,

> We didn't want someone who desired to retire with a gold watch. We wanted entrepreneurs, demonstrated winners, high-energy contributors who defined their previous role in terms of what they contributed and not what their titles were. . . . I fought with some managers who wanted to fill a role quickly to get a project moving, but if it took six months to find the best, they'd have to wait. We looked for people who had an energy for creating something new. Our motto was "Surprise me."[6]

Recruiting the right people, relating to them in meaningful ways day in and day out and providing honest, candid feedback, not just criticism, will extend both a leader's influence and tenure.

Years ago I had a senior administrator, one of the vice presidents of the university, come to my office completely frustrated with a key student leader. The VP said, "I'm not going to talk to her again. She has a different agenda and doesn't want to cooperate, so I'm just not going to meet with her again."

After listening and allowing him to express his frustration, I said, "The only problem with your decision is that you *have* to work with her, like it or not. She is the student representative. So please hold steady, take the high road, and continue to meet with her." I suggested that he may wish to enlist a few other students with whom he had a good relationship to participate in the planning sessions with him and the student leader in question in hopes that they could aid in tempering this particular student's agenda. Leaders lead leaders, and that can be challenging.

4. What has not changed for you during your time at Hallmark?

As Brad reflected on his long career at Hallmark, his face brightened as he said, "My respect for those I work for and with has not changed from day one. This is a great company, and my respect for the core values of the company has remained constant through all the various changes we have encountered across the years. If those things weren't true, I'd leave. I simply have to believe in the company and in the people with whom I work."

"Thankfully, I have also been able to maintain a balance between my work, which is very demanding, and my life outside of work." Moore's career demonstrates that balance between work and non-work is very important and, perhaps counter-intuitively, adds both years and greater productivity to one's work.

5. Have there been any particular challenges or new initiatives along the way that have helped renew your effectiveness as a leader?

Among the various assignments Moore has had with Hallmark, he stated that his work as head of advertising and promotion and his international work stretched him professionally and required significant time management improvements for him. He also noted that one of his most challenging assignments was to lead Hallmark's publishing subsidiary at a particularly stressful time. When he took that assignment, changing media realities were forcing publishers to close down numerous magazines—ranging from relatively new ones to others that had been thriving for decades. *Hallmark Magazine,* despite its outstanding quality, had to be discontinued. "That old chestnut about learning more from failure than from success? Well, it's true," he says. "That wasn't the first time I experienced it, and I'm sure it won't be the last."Knowing that identifying Brad as an avid motorcyclist is an understatement, I also asked,

6. Any leadership lessons from the world of motorcycling?

I particularly loved his first response to this question. "Stay on the road," he said. Then he added, "And stay on your side of the road. I've failed miserably at high speed and with near-fatal crashes—but I survived."

I know that Brad's ride from the southern tip of South America was particularly difficult, but he made it. There is something about the ability of a leader to just keep going, even in the face of difficulty.

He also noted, "Plan where you're going *before* starting up and getting in gear. You can't open a map as easily on a motorcycle as you can in a car. And a GPS is harder to use too." In leadership, as well as motorcycling, one needs not only a strong sense of direction but also the ability to determine and plot out each leg of the journey before setting off toward a distant and perhaps difficult destination.

Brad added this comment, which is also a key to good leadership: "When you see a really great road, it's probably worth trying if you have the time or at least remembering to come back later." Leaders should not be so focused on a particular destination that they miss an opportunity along the way.

STEVE JOBS' JOB

With the relatively recent passing of Steve Jobs, the founder and force behind Apple, his leadership legacy has become a publishing industry all its own, led by the masterful biography *Steve Jobs*, by award-winning writer Walter Isaacson. There is much about Jobs that one would not want to emulate; but he was driven by a set of principles that can be helpful to anyone in leadership. In the book *The Innovation Secrets of Steve Jobs*, Camine Gallo identifies seven of those principles as follows:[7]

Principle One: Do what you love.

Steve Jobs was a college dropout. He attended Reed College in Portland, Oregon, for a semester but could not see the point in it. "I had no idea what I wanted to do with my life and no idea how college was going to help me figure it out. So I decided to drop out and trust that it would all work out OK."[8] He chose to follow his heart; if he didn't love it, he didn't want to do it. Certainly not everyone is wired that way, but the idea is transferable for leaders who stay with the same work over many years. They must love what they do if they are to last.

In an interview recorded as part of the Smithsonian Oral History Project, Jobs spoke of the link between passion and perseverance:

> I think you should go get a job as a busboy or something until you find something you're really passionate about, be-

cause it's a lot of work. I'm convinced that about half of what separates the successful entrepreneurs from the non-successful ones is pure perseverance. It is so hard . . . unless you have a lot of passion about this. You're not going to survive. You are going to give up.[9]

In a 2005 commencement address at Stanford University, he said, "Your job is limited, so don't waste it living someone else's life."[10]

Principle Two: Put a dent in the universe.

"Put a dent in the universe" was one of Steve Jobs' favorite sayings, particularly as he was developing the Macintosh computer. The way he made his various "dents" was primarily through innovation more than invention. He did not invent the personal computer or the MP3 player; but his innovations, the Mac and Ipod, "re-invented" those things and sparked a revolution. His experience illustrates that a leader who can innovate, do the new thing, and adapt to a new reality is a leader who will last. "Steve has a power of vision that is almost frightening," observed Trip Hawkins, a former vice president at Apple.[11] "When Steve believes in something, the power of that vision can literally sweep aside any objections or problems. They just cease to exist."

This approach seems to suggest that one should embrace vision rather than mission. A clear sense of mission is vital, particularly for long-term leadership. It provides ballast and buoyancy through the years; yet it is vision that adds energy and attracts followers.

Principle Three: Kick-start your brain.

"Kick-start your brain" is an odd phrase by which Jobs was saying to think differently—put your brain in a different gear, and you will arrive at a different outcome. He understood creativity as the simple act of connecting, making connections that others overlook or underestimate. Jobs went well beyond imitating others—he had the capacity of looking at what others had done or were doing and perceive a new reality. "Jobs doesn't just *see* things differently from the rest of us. Jobs *perceives* things differently."[12]

Kick-starting one's brain has to do with how a person interprets what he or she sees. Leaders think differently about how they think—they look for the edge, for the gap, for the missing link, for the "so-what" and the "what-next." Einstein said that imagination was more important than knowledge. Good leaders learn to question the status quo.

Principle Four: Sell dreams, not products.

Selling dreams, not products, was particularly important to the success of Apple computers. A popular Apple ad from a year or so ago stated, "The people who are crazy enough to think they can change the world are the ones who do."

At the university we often talk about selling the myth of going to college. This is a phrase that takes time to fully appreciate. Think about a college view book or web page. The images are those that most naturally come to mind when one thinks about going to college: a great campus, classrooms and labs filled with eager students surrounding a teacher in a crisp lab coat, the marching band on parade, scenes from the dining hall or the snack shop, a candid photo of students lost in conversation in a crowded dorm room, the soccer team celebrating a goal. Every college or university is trying to tap into the idea of the ideal—to convince prospective students that their dreams of college can be a reality on this campus. In a way, all salespeople sell dreams rather than products.

The implication of this idea for leaders is to underscore the role of a compelling narrative. Most people want to link their personal life stories with an overarching story line that adds significance and meaning to their work.

Principle Five: Say no to one thousand things.

Jobs said, "I'm as proud of what we don't do as I am of what we do." He realized that for Apple to excel it would need to simplify and focus. When Apple unveiled the iPhone in January 2007, its simplicity was one of its finest features. Most phone manufacturers were in the process of adding more and more buttons and features to their phones. Jobs and his crew went the other direction. The iPhone was a study in minimalism plus.

The design and operating concept was very simply: one button and a bright, colorful screen. Yet it could do more, not less, than the others on the market. The Apple goal was to make the phone "super-easy to use." Like a fine architect, Jobs believed less is more. That principle shows up repeatedly in the Apple products: iPod, iPhone, and the Mac. Gallo writes, "It takes courage to be innovative, especially if you decide to eliminate clutter in favor of a focused, simple, elegant design."[13]

Principle Six: Create insanely great experiences.

Across the many years that Steve Jobs' influence fueled the Apple revolution, the organization focused not just on products or sales but also on experiences for their customers. The Macintosh was designed to provide a different, more engaging experience for its users than the IBM personal computer could deliver. And the Apple stores were not just stores—they were resource centers and hands-on computer labs. Apple stores are magnetic. The company opened its first retail store in 2001, and in fewer than five years reached five billion dollars in annual sales, reaching that mark faster than any other retailer in history.

One way a leader can re-vision, and thus renew, his or her leadership is to foster meaningful experiences along the way. When we opened our most recent major building on campus, a 168,000-square-foot student life and recreation center, we didn't just let people wander in and start using the building as it was completed or simply hold a traditional ribbon-cutting ceremony. We wanted something more dramatic.

The completion date for this building was scheduled for December; so the official opening event for the new building was scheduled for just after midnight at 12:12 on December 12, 2012. This idea sparked a level of interest among the students—as well as the faculty and staff—that could not have been achieved by way of a traditional opening. There were balloons, a band, food, tours, and lots of recreation well into the early hours of the morning. The building was designed to foster community and provide recreation and socialization for a growing student body, and the grand opening sent all the right signals—this was the place to be!

Principle Seven: Master the message.

The final principle that sustained Jobs' legacy was his showman-like ability to master the message. He could convince others that his latest idea was a great idea—not just another version or variation of something already available. He was a storyteller and salesman whose understated presentations carried the weight of his own conviction. Carmine Gallo writes,

> Companies, executives, and entrepreneurs around the world are trying to deconstruct the magic behind Apple's success. They take apart Apple's products to learn clues about their unique designs. They study Steve Jobs for clues to his thinking. Each of the components is a part of the story . . . but the seventh principle . . . may be most important. Steve Jobs has mastered the message, communicating his ideas so brilliantly that he persuades investors, employees, and customers to back his vision and to join him on his journey.[14]

Part of the secret of renewal through messaging is to think and present visually. Images communicate feelings as well as information. The best way for me to tell the Olivet story is to show the picture of a student rather than talk about accreditation visits, the number of majors and minors, or educational theories. The student is at the heart of why we exist and what we do. It would be unusual for the university to host a donor event or a board meeting or community gathering without involving students in the programs. They are the message.

11
RE
SIST

*Your present circumstances don't determine where you can go;
they merely determine where you start.*
—Nido Qubein

*The dream and the dreamer are always matched.
You could not have a dream without the means, right now, to begin it.*
—Marta Davidovich Ockuly

Henry Jekyll was an upright, respectable, Victorian English gentleman. He was moral and honest and reliable. He was industrious and restrained in all his behavior—a model citizen in every respect. Yet deep within him resided an alter ego, a second personality, a persona that was released and empowered by the use of a self-administered drug: a kind of potion, a mood altering, personality-changing concoction that had been developed secretly by Dr. Jekyll. When used, it transformed him into a much different person—one who assumed the name Mr. Edward Hyde.

The story of Dr. Jekyll and Mr. Hyde is a story that can be read at several levels. Older children like it because it is an adventure story, and they enjoy the mystery and drama. But at an adult level it is another kind of story. It is the story of the impulses, drives, obsessions, and compulsions of what someone has called "the shadow self."

It was Carl Jung, psychiatrist and writer, who coined that phrase, saying that within every woman and every man there exists a person no one else sees or knows, a "shadow self."

Robert Louis Stevenson's story of Dr. Jekyll and Mr. Hyde is a story of the battle one man had with this inner shadow self. Dr. Henry Jekyll, in his "full statement" at the end of the story, tells how he would, through the use of this secret potion, give himself over to the full expression of evil, which was made visible in the person of Mr. Hyde. Dr. Jekyll tells how he could, in the beginning, overcome that alter ego and could lay to rest that evil nature again by the use of this drug.

It is a frightening story in many ways, for at the end Dr. Jekyll begins to lose control of the process and becomes powerless to keep the evil Mr. Hyde restrained. The good that he wants to do is overpowered by the evil influence of Mr. Hyde. The story ends with Dr. Jekyll's life being totally destroyed by the power of this "other" self.

Why refer to such a story as this?

Every leader lives in the midst of a tug-of-war, not usually between good and evil but often between competing priorities and pressures. Part of a leader's job is to balance the centrifugal forces of institutional life that tend to pull an organization apart—forces of individuality, academic freedom, cultural changes, economic issues, and so on, against the centripetal forces that tend to preserve the integrity and unity of the organization, things like mission, morale, vision, progress, and community. This dynamic tension calls for a new understanding of what it takes to make an organization run. Leaders must resist the strong pull of business as usual.

With rapidly changing technology, a downsized workforce, and an emphasis on acquiring a broad range of skills, leaders today have to be more flexible than ever in their roles. Taking risks in their approach to management is the only choice left for those who want to have an impact on an increasingly global workforce.[1]

This strikes at the heart of the important distinction between management and leadership, or to use the Joiner and Josephs' leadership agility model—between Achiever and Catalyst. The important distinction between leadership and management was first publicly articulated by Warren Bennis in a speech at the Federal Executive Institute. Bennis, of course, is now considered one of the nation's foremost authorities on leadership.

His distinction between leadership and management originally grew out of his personal experience in higher education. He served for a time as the president of the University of Cincinnati. Less than a year into that job, overwhelmed and faced with a nearly endless mass of papers and problems, he began to realize that he was so enmeshed caring for the administrative details and responding to the various stakeholders that he was unable to launch the initiatives needed to advance a new vision for the school. He realized that he was managing the university but not leading it.

Effective leaders come to realize that they must do both—manage and lead. The art of it all stems from finding the right balance at the right time in the right measure. There are some stretches of time when the president or CEO of an organization will do little more than manage—problem-solve, reorganize, evaluate, and supervise. But there must also be regular and sustained times when the dominant note sounded by the CEO is one of leadership.

Resisting the press of the daily demands or the call of the urgent in order to focus on the next new thing is an important part of the re-visioning process. My father was a businessman and entrepreneur. Starting with nothing more than desire, he built a fine newspaper and commercial printing business. Near the end of his career he owned nine newspapers and ran two shifts daily in the production area, where his plan was to keep the presses rolling, printing scores of other jobs during the "off hours" when they were not printing the newspapers.

He was busy building the business when I was a teenager, and I remember that from time to time he went to the office on weekends, saying, "I need some looking-out-the-window time." I had no idea what he was talking about. Now I realize that what he needed was time for reflection and particularly for planning and envisioning his next strategic moves in building the business.

SOUTHWEST AIRLINES

Any way you look at it, Southwest Airlines is a prototype for any company wishing to establish a consistent record of growth and constant adaptation. When Southwest started operations on June 8, 1971, their prospects were dim. The vision and business plan for the airline, initially sketched on a cocktail napkin in a San Antonio restaurant nearly five years before, met with immediate and strong resistance, particularly from their competition, forcing Southwest Airlines into litigation with them for more than four years before it could operate its first flight—including one case that made it all the way to the United States Supreme Court and three others to the Texas Supreme Court. Most would have given up. Southwest did not.

The initial business plan was to fly solely intrastate, linking the three major cities in Texas: Dallas/Ft Worth, Houston, and San Antonio—the golden triangle of Texas. Gary Kelly, the current president and CEO of Southwest noted, "If you were one of the few Southwest customers back in 1971, you pretty much had the flight to yourself. We even had to discontinue weekend service for a while due to lack of passengers. It's amazing that we survived those times."[2]

Herb Kelleher, the founder and chairman emeritus of Southwest, wrote, "From our operational inception through today, Southwest has been an innovative leader in the airline industry."[3]

The Southwest story is not just about a bold and persistent startup; the true magic of the story lies in the nearly constant re-visioning of the company across the years that enabled it to survive the turbulence of the airline industry that grounded giants like Pan Am and forced most of the other major carriers to file bankruptcy and reorganize through a series of mergers and corporate partnership and alliances.

By the time Southwest Airlines was celebrating its fortieth anniversary, the company's fleet of planes had grown from three to five hundred fifty one, and its annual originating customers from one hundred eight thousand in 1971 to more than eighty-eight million in 2010. The anniversary issue of Southwest's flight magazine featured a story titled "40 Lessons to Learn from Southwest."

Among those lessons are these:

- Keep the idea simple enough to draw on a napkin.
- Hire a good lawyer.
- Raise more money than you think you will need. Now double it.
- Target the overcharged and underserved.
- Be the good guy.
- Promote from within.
- Invent your own culture, and put a top person in charge of it.
- A culture has its own language.

- A crisis can contain the germ of a big idea.
- Remember your chief mission.
- Simplicity has value. The airline has a simple fare structure and flies only one type of aircraft, the Boeing 737. Keep it simple.
- Take your business, not yourself, seriously.
- See your business as a cause.
- Put the worker first. No wonder Southwest received more than one hundred thousand applications in 2012 for just over two thousand job openings.
- Set and renew noble expectations.
- Manage permanence. Many talk about the importance of managing change, but it is equally important to know what not to change.
- Never rest on your laurels.[4]

FIFTEEN PAIRS OF SHOES

I mentioned earlier of taking a tour of western Turkey. Our guide for those days was a Muslim gentleman named Huzur who throughout the week was observing the Islamic holy days called Ramadan. During one of our conversations he said that his wife had asked our small group to pray for her because she had a tough decision to make.

The next day he gathered us around again and with great excitement told us the following story. Having talked with his wife once more, she told him that she had felt compelled, as part of her observance of the holy days, to buy a pair of shoes for a needy child at the school where she was a teacher. She had requested prayer so that she would be able to choose with wisdom which child should get those shoes, for there were more than a dozen needy children in her class. She finally settled on a young boy from a particularly impoverished family.

Later that day she stopped by a shoe merchant and found a pair of shoes, but she was unsure of the boy's shoe size. Not wanting to tell the merchant why she was buying these shoes—because acts of charity are to be done privately—she simply asked, "If these shoes are not the right size, may I return them for another pair?"

"Oh, yes," he said. "That will be fine. But may I ask a favor of you?"

"Yes," Huzur's wife replied.

"I would like to make a gift to the poor," the merchant said quietly. "You are a teacher—would you help me?"

"If I can, I will surely do it," she responded.

The man stepped to the back of his little shop and returned in a moment with fifteen pairs of shoes, which he gave to her to distribute. There were enough for all the needy children in her class.

As the teacher resisted certain dynamics that would have kept her from being generous, such as the cost involved, the confusion concerning which child should get the shoes, the uncertainty of the size and so on, it set the stage for an even greater act of charity on the part of the shopkeeper. The teacher's seemingly small act of giving was catalytic. Re-visioning can often set in motion a ripple of change as one person or one department models the desired behaviors or outcomes. Sometimes individuals need to see the change before they can embrace it.

Trying to gain a vision of the future is not an easy task.

- In 1926 Lee de Forest, inventor of the cathode ray tube, stated, "Television may seem feasible, but from a practical standpoint, I consider it an improbability—a development which we should waste little time dreaming about."
- In 1943 Thomas J. Watson, Chairman of the Board of IBM, noted in a report to the board of directors, "I think there is a world market for about five computers."

- In 1962 a music recording expert in Great Britain was quoted in a trade magazine as saying, "We don't think the Beatles will have much of an impact in the popular market. In fact, guitar groups are on their way out."[5]

When it comes to gazing into the future, leaders may frequently "see through a glass darkly." Yet leaders are nearly always men and women of the future. Leaders who provide continuity and progress over long periods of time learn to resist the pull of the past and all the seemingly apparent reasons something won't work in favor of why it may work.

IT'S HOT DOWN HERE

I heard a story not long ago during a particularly cold spell of a Minneapolis couple who impulsively decided to go to Florida for a long weekend to thaw out and get a break from the frigid weather. They planned to stay at the same hotel where they had spent their honeymoon twenty years earlier. Because of their hectic schedules and the fact that the trip was a last-minute idea, it was difficult to coordinate their travel plans.

So the husband left Minnesota and flew to Florida on Thursday, with his wife planning to fly down the following day. The husband checked into the hotel, and everything was terrific, just as he had remembered; in fact, it was better. There was a computer in his room, so he decided to send an e-mail to his wife. However, somehow he accidentally left out one letter in her e-mail address, and without realizing his error, he sent the note.

Meanwhile, somewhere in Houston, a widow had just returned home from her husband's funeral. He was a minister who was called home to heaven following a heart attack. The widow decided to check her e-mail, expecting messages from relatives and friends who could not attend the service. After reading the first message, she screamed and fainted.

The widow's son rushed into the room, found his mother on the floor, and saw a message on the computer screen that read—

To: My Loving Wife

Subject: I've arrived

Date: January 20, 2007

I know you must be surprised to hear from me. They have computers here now, and you are allowed to send e-mails to your loved ones. I've just arrived and have been checked in. I see that everything has been prepared for your arrival tomorrow. Looking forward to seeing you then! Hope your journey is as uneventful as mine.

Your loving husband

P.S. Sure is hot down here.[6]

There may be some surprises along the way; most leaders encounter the unexpected or misperceptions as they chart a course to the future. When such moments come, leaders need to hold steady, clarify the issues at hand, and communicate effectively to all who might be impacted. The stable presence of a leader, on site and in touch, can stabilize times of stress and misunderstanding.

THE POWER OF PRESENCE

Addressing the 2012 graduating seniors, I opened my remarks with these words:

Last fall, not long after school started here at Olivet, a social movement began in lower Manhattan. It was understood as a reaction to what the protestors believed was an unjust and broken social and financial system. These protestors camped out in Zucotti Park near the financial hub of Wall Street.

They demonstrated, blocked traffic, carried signs, chanted slogans, and garnered the attention of the press. The movement was quickly known as "Occupy Wall Street."

Before long, the effort spread to other cities and other countries as well. The movement rested on an understanding of the power of presence: occupy, show up, make a statement simply by being there. My purpose this evening is not to reflect positively or negatively on that effort but to call you as young women and men to a different, though somewhat similar, movement. For I, too, believe in the power of presence.

Tomorrow you will graduate from Olivet Nazarene University. For the past several years you have "occupied" this campus, but after tomorrow you will begin to occupy hundreds of other places. You will show up and make a statement by simply being there.

My central question for you this evening is this: what difference will your presence make: In that distant city where you will live, in the office where you will work, in the hospital where you will care for patients, in classrooms where you will teach, in neighborhoods, graduate schools, churches, apartment buildings, coffee shops, and restaurants—what difference will your presence make?

My desire for you, and the great need of our world, is that regardless of where you live or what you do, the passion of your life would be as salt and light in a dark and decaying world. The world that waits for you, on the other side of graduation, is a complicated and unsettled world. There are war and terror. There are economic instability and job insecurity. There's an upside-down view of what is right and wrong, moral or immoral, acceptable and unacceptable. There is a sea of broken human relationships out there. And you will have to find your place in that wide-open-anything-goes-nothing-is-shocking-anymore society.

There is a power in presence, and certainly a leader's presence makes a difference. Just showing up to engage in the conversation and ask the right questions and encourage others will help overcome the tendency within organizations not to change. Leaders are by definition change agents. They are catalytic. Effective leaders instill hope and optimism, even in the face of obstacles.

MONOPOLY

Beginning in the fall of 1929, the United States and much of the industrialized world entered into the Great Depression. The stock market plunged, businesses failed, people panicked. In place after place folks rushed to their banks only to find the word "closed" written across their futures. The ripple of hardship spread quickly from America's great cities to the small towns of its heartland to the abandoned farms of the dust bowl.

It was a desperate time in many ways; there was high unemployment, pervasive poverty, soup lines, and the establishment of the government-sponsored Works Progress Administration, W.P.A. For many, as they began dealing with the reality of a long and deep economic downturn, the financial depression soon gave way to an emotional depression.

On the East Coast two brothers named Parker had managed to survive the initial days of the Depression with a small financial nest egg. But as the Depression began to drag on, it became clear to them that unless they found a way to increase their funds, they, too, would soon be destitute.

They considered various options; should they try the stock market, should they buy land or start a new business? After considering these possibilities and several others, they decided to produce and market a game—a family game. This seemed incredible and particularly risky to their friends, but the Parker brothers were convinced of their idea. They put what money they had into the development and production of this idea.

Soon, to everyone's amazement but their own, all across America people began buying this new game. Folks would play by the hours. People who hardly knew when or if their next paycheck was coming could, as they played the game, hold hundreds of dollars in their hands. Individuals who struggled to pay the rent could, for a couple of hours, own houses and hotels.

Young people who had not yet been away from home could nonetheless stay for a while on the Boardwalk of Atlantic City or ride the Reading Railroad. Before long there was hardly a household in America who didn't own a Monopoly game—by the Parker Brothers. How do you explain this? Money so tight, yet, people still bought a game.

I think part of the answer is this: the game of Monopoly provided a kind of artificial ray of hope in the midst of desperate times. It was an avenue to move beyond the grim realities of the Great Depression to the promise of a better day. While it was just a game, it was good medicine for the spirit.

Warren Bennis calls it "inventing a life." In the preface to his fine book *An Invented Life*, he tells about growing up with two older brothers, identical twins. After telling a little about each of the brothers, he writes, "My brothers taught me the first two things I learned about leadership: (1) that it is a function of character as well as behavior (now that's my point exactly) and (2) that leading is better than following.[7]

Max Depree noted that we cannot become what we need to be by remaining what we are. I have observed that too many people are interested in making a success *in* life rather than making a success *of* life. They overvalue what they have and undervalue what they are. Don't give in to that temptation.

Part of the ongoing challenge to excellence is this idea that Warren Bennis introduces—the idea of inventing oneself. At first I didn't like the sound of this. "Inventing oneself" sounded as though one were to manufacture a persona or take on an image of something one is not.

But as I read Bennis's book and thought about it, I realized it was just the opposite. Rather than inventing something we're not, we are to invent something we *are*. The basic idea is simple self-determination. The challenge is to face the strengths, weaknesses, opportunities, and obstacles of your life and determine who you are going to be—invent yourself.

Bennis writes, "People who cannot invent and reinvent themselves must be content with borrowed postures, secondhand ideas, fitting in instead of standing out. Inventing oneself is the opposite of accepting the roles we were brought up to play.[8]

That's good. Too many people are playing to the crowd in the stands, acting out a role, a set of expectations they believe others have for them rather than determining for themselves who they are and committing themselves fully to be that person.

To be authentic is literally to be your own author. One can hear the same root word at work—*authentic/author.* We are to write our own story rather than live someone else's. You can be who you want to be, maybe not *what* you want to be, fully—I understand the limitations of life. But within those limitations, we individuals can invent ourselves.

This process does not happen in isolation—you don't take a day off, go away someplace, invent yourself, and come back as a new person. No, I think the inventing of oneself and the charting of one's course to excellence happens in the midst of life, in the midst of living.

A PROPER UNDERSTANDING OF FAILURE

Failure is, in a sense, the highway to success, inasmuch as every discovery of what is false leads us to seek earnestly after what is true. Don't be afraid of failure. I do not know a person who is excellent at anything who has not failed along the way. Failure is not final—only quitting is final.

This was reinforced in my thinking as I watched the funeral service for President Richard Nixon. I was particularly taken with a quotation included in the remarks of California Governor Pete Wilson. The original quote from the Greek philosopher Sophocles was this: "One must wait until the evening to see how splendid the day has been."

Governor Wilson applied that observation to the life of President Nixon. There is insight here for us all. The real test of our effort is the test of time. Things may look one way in the morning, another way at noon, but "One must wait until the evening to see how splendid the day has been."

In the pursuit of excellence we must learn to overcome our failures. That is hard to do if you define yourself simply in terms of performance, but if you define excellence in terms of who you are and not just what you do, then failure need not be final.

THE CHECKERED FLAG

Each May a green flag drops at the Indianapolis Motor Speedway signaling the start of one of the world's most celebrated races. Thirty-three gleaming turbocharged autos shoot out of the fourth turn and roar past the starting line at over two hundred miles per hour. What a sight!

On the pace lap and the first few racing laps, every car looks great and is running strong. However, people who follow Indy every year understand that the goal is not just to start well but to finish well. Give the race a little time, and as in past years, a toll will start to be taken. Engine failure, tire problems, and a host of other calamities will befall car after car until perhaps as many as one-half of the cars that start the race will fail to finish it.

It is hard to overemphasize the importance of finishing well. Trophies rarely get handed to those who simply cross the starting line. The prize and the money go only to those who cross the *finish* line.

What does it take to finish the race, to succeed in your professional/career commitments, your family priorities, your faith commitments, and your pursuit of excellence?

Every racer at Indianapolis knows that—

1. No one wins who does not enter. One might be the best race car driver the world has ever seen, but this person will not win unless he or she races. Everything else flows from that point of entering. So whether it is business or family or faith—you have to try.

2. Each driver must stay on course. The race is a five-hundred-mile race, but that does not mean that a driver can drive from Indianapolis to Louisville and back and expect to win the prize. It is not a race of five hundred miles in any direction. It is not five hundred miles in a straight line. It is a race over a prescribed course, and if one does not stay on course, he or she cannot win the race. It seems to me that Americans have lost sight of this basic concept—staying on course. We can't even agree as to what the course is, much less commit ourselves to it.

3. The drivers also know that they must follow the rules of the race. One cannot suddenly decide to go the opposite direction on the oval track, or perhaps stop in the middle of turn three to stretch his or her legs or check the oil. These things will lead to disqualification—or worse. The rules are not there to hamper the race but to enhance it. Enter the race, stay on course, and obey the rules.

4. Watch for the checkered flag. Individuals run well when they keep the goal always before them. James Allen said, "You will become as small as your controlling desire or as great as your dominate aspiration." Leaders strive not only to start well but also to finish well; that is when the checkered flag drops. Their eyes look to the horizon. It is at the horizon one first encounters daybreak: a hint of light, the soft stir of a morning breeze, a gentle freshness in the air. These all signal a new beginning.

The horizon is the place where tomorrow begins, the point where the past gives way to the future, where shadows are dispelled in the bright white light of a new day. And thus, the horizon can be a place that renews one's spirit. Dag Hammarskjold, former Secretary General of the United Nations, wrote, "Never look down to test the ground before taking your next step; only he who keeps his eye fixed upon the far horizon will find the right road."[9]

12
RE
NEW

I have always been delighted at the prospect of a new day,
a fresh try, one more start, with perhaps a bit of magic
waiting somewhere behind the morning.
—J. B. Priestly

Baby step by baby step, you have what you need right now to
start moving in the direction of your happiest dreams.
—Marta Davidovich Ockuly

The long, steady process of re-visioning culminates in the renewal of an organization and the individual who leads it. A leader's ability and commitment to renew each aspect of his or her work and each dynamic of organizational life fuel and sustain the re-vision process. This helps to counter the natural tendency to focus on the wrong things. Too often leaders confuse what is of highest value with that which is only marginally valuable. In those cases, leaders manage the bottom line rather than driving the top line and caring for the individuals whose work makes the organization functional.

HAROLD AND EMMA

Harold and Emma had been married for nearly sixty years. One afternoon as they visited the state fair, Harold noticed a sign for helicopter rides. That was one thing, he told Emma, that he surely would like to do someday. So they walked over to the helicopter to take a look.

Emma asked the pilot, "How much do you charge?"

"Fifty dollars for fifteen minutes," he replied.

She said to Harold, "That's pretty expensive, but why don't you go on and take a ride? You've always wanted to do it."

Harold replied, "Oh, Darlin'—we can't afford it. Remember: fifty dollars is fifty dollars. I'll just wait till next year."

The pilot overheard them talking and said, "Sir, I will make you a deal. I will take you and your wife up for a ride and will not charge you a cent—as long as you don't make a sound. But if you yell or call out, then you will owe me the fifty dollars."

Emma and Harold agreed.

Once the helicopter was airborne, the pilot began to do a series of sharp turns and other rather dramatic maneuvers, but Harold never said a word. The pilot tried once more to get his passengers to make a sound, but he could not. Once they had landed, the pilot turned to Harold and said, "I can't believe you did not make a sound all that time."

"Well, to tell you the truth, I almost said something when Emma fell out—but fifty dollars is fifty dollars."

PLAY BALL!

From time to time when I get weary of the daily routines of life, I rearrange my schedule, slip into my car, and drive north on Interstate 57. I follow that ribbon of road until it merges with the great Dan Ryan Expressway on the south side of Chicago.

I am swept along briskly with the early afternoon traffic into the heart of the city. I exit and make my way around the edge of downtown. On one side of me are towering buildings gleaming in the sun, and on the other side are the cool waters of Lake Michigan. Little by little I make my way to the near north side, where I park my car a block or two from my destination and walk the remaining distance to 1060 West Addison Street.

I enter a line and wait my turn. Arriving at the window. I declare my intentions, "One, please," and slide my money to a faceless, voiceless person, who without comment hands me a ticket. I check the numbers and begin looking for my entrance.

Finding the gate, I enter and am transported from the foreboding, real world on the outside into the inviting surrealistic world of daytime baseball at Wrigley Field, home of the Chicago Cubs. For the next couple of hours I am in a world that is defined by exactly measured lines and precise geometric patterns. It is a wonderful place where nearly every motion on the playing field is graceful and poised. Sloppy behavior is not tolerated. Here is a world where outstanding performance is recognized and applauded on the spot.

Errors are instantly detected and their consequences immediately experienced. Rule infractions are punished directly. Unruly conduct is banished. The person who refuses to play by the rules is ejected.

While the game is being played I look around me. People, thousands of people, people of widely divergent cultural and social backgrounds, with differing temperaments, moral standards, religious commitments, all watching. All are in agreement as to the rules and the goal of the game.

When the game is over, everyone knows who won and who lost. It is so precise that afterward the radio announcers can describe the entire experience in the stark vocabulary of numbers—exact to the third decimal point: batting averages, ERAs, and so on.

But then I am forced to leave that world and return to the world outside, the world where we live, the world in which we work and raise families. In doing so, I observe this: the world to which I return after the game contains all the same elements that were visible in the stadium—competition, performance, error, reward, ambition, boundary, risk, failure, relationships, indolence, and excellence.

It's all here, but with a significant difference. Instead of being sharply distinguished, all these aspects of life are hopelessly muddled. None of the lines is precise. The boundaries are not always clear. Goals are not easily agreed upon. Performance is measured too often with a sliding scale.

When I leave the world of brightly colored geometric patterns, I return to the real world of odd shapes and irregularity, where winning and losing are issues that are often painfully hard to determine. When do we ever get thousands of people to watch our performance and agree on the stated goal, the rules of conduct, and level of accomplishment?

In this world we are left to determine meaning as best we can. In such a world, we need a clear sense of our core values as individuals and as an organization. It is our value system that becomes our internal umpire in a world that often refuses to play by the rules.

This reality underscores the need to pause from time to time, as individuals and as an organization, to take inventory and to review our mission, vision, and values.

Many years ago, on the day I was installed as president of Olivet, I was given a plaque. At the top was a copy of the invitation to my inauguration ceremony, and at the bottom was an extended quote from Robert Coles, with whom I had studied briefly at Harvard. The quotation was from his book *Harvard Diary: Reflections on the Sacred and the Secular*. This quote is found in a section in which he is talking about an interview he had with a young woman who worked for a time in one of the departments of Harvard, where unfortunately she was mistreated.

He writes—

She gradually began to realize how much she had learned without question, the hard way. She began to realize that being clever, brilliant, even what gets called "well-educated" is not to be equated, necessarily, with being considerate, kind, tactful, even plain polite or civil. She began to realize that one's proclaimed social or political views—however articulately humanitarian—are not always guarantors of one's everyday behavior. One can write lofty editorials and falter badly in one's moral life. One can speak big-hearted words, write incisive and thoughtful prose—and be a rather crude, arrogant, smug person in the course of getting through a day.[1]

Character, my father used to tell me, is what you're like when no one's watching you—or, I guess, when you forget that others are watching.[2]

INTEGRITY

If you have integrity, nothing else matters. If you don't have integrity, nothing else matters. To reach a great height, a person needs to have great depth.

William Shakespeare wrote, "To thine own self be true, and it must follow, as the night the day, thou canst not then be false to any man.[3]

Integrity involves a consistency of actions, values, methods, measures, principles, expectations, and outcomes. In ethics, integrity is regarded as honesty and truthfulness. The word "integrity" stems from the Latin idea of *whole* or *complete*. In this context, integrity is the inner sense of "wholeness" deriving from qualities such as honesty and consistency of character. As such, one may judge that others "have integrity" to the extent that they act according to the values, beliefs, and principles that they claim to hold.

ASTROLOGY

Years ago, long before the birth of the scientific method, before printed books and mass communication and long before telescopes and so on, men and women became fascinated with the sky. They noticed the power of the sun and soon began to worship it as a great fiery god. Then they turned their attention to the moon—mysterious phases, tides, planting, harvesting cycles, and so on.

They wondered—if the sun was a god by day and the moon by night, then what about the stars? The nighttime sky was filled with lights and wonders. As they gazed into the heavens, they began to see pictures, clusters of stars that seemed to represent certain things: a lion, a scorpion, a bull, a fish, an archer, a water carrier, a set of twins, a virgin maiden, and so on.

One of the interesting things about these constellations is that they would move in a predictable pattern across the sky, with one of the twelve clusters of stars moving to a place of ascendancy at the "top" of the heavens, so to speak, and remain there for a month or so, then give way to another constellation for the following month.

The speculation was that if one was born while a particular cluster of stars ruled the heavens, then those stars would continue to have a certain power and influence over an individual's life. From these observations, a whole theory called astrology developed with its elaborate understanding of the signs of the Zodiac.

When I was in seminary, I worked one summer in a hospital—a large city hospital—in the heart of Ft. Worth, Texas. I worked the third shift, which meant I went to work at eleven o'clock at night and got off at seven the next morning.

The first night I was there I was given an orientation and taken around to the various departments to meet some of the other staff. The one individual who continues to stand out in my memory of that place more than any other is a woman who served as the head nurse in the emergency room. With all due respect to fine nurses everywhere, I must say that a head nurse in an emergency room on the midnight shift in a large city hospital is, by definition, one tough character.

When I was escorted on that first night to the emergency room to meet the head nurse, I said, "Hello." But she just stood there and looked at me. I smiled self-consciously, nodded a little, cleared my throat, and shifted my weight from one foot to the other. Still just staring at me, she finally said, "What's your sign?"

I instinctively looked down at the badge, the name tag, I was wearing.

"When were you born?" she barked.

"January thirteenth."

"You're a Capricorn." she declared. "You're a goat," she added with some sense of authority.

About this time, I began to think of some animals of which she reminded me. But of course, I didn't say anything. She didn't give me a chance. "You are a Capricorn, a mountain goat; you are a climber, sure-footed and cautious." On she went for a few moments giving me an initial astrological evaluation.

When she finished, I said, "Nice to meet you," and slipped away.

Throughout that summer I saw employees from nearly all departments of the hospital slipping down to the emergency room for a "consultation" with this lady. Some would not make a major decision without checking with her.

Why do people believe in such things as astrology? There may be a variety of reasons, among them the desire to have some help in knowing how to chart the course of life and work and family. For organizations, leaders must meet that need to have direction and find purpose and meaning in the ordinary aspects of work and organizational life. It is the renewal of one's values and vision rather than the stars that shape an organization's identity and influence. A renewed organizational vision has a strong impact on the attitudes of personnel throughout the organization.

"I'm going to be sad today."

A father was having breakfast with his family. He and his wife had been scurrying around getting themselves ready for work and the children ready for school. As they finally sat together for a few moments, the youngest child, a little first-grade boy, announced with a cheerful smile, "I'm going to be sad today."

The father responded, "You're going to be sad today?"

"Yes," the little fellow chirped.

"Why do you want to be sad today?" his father asked.

"Because when you're sad at school, all the teachers take turns giving you a hug."

Everyone from the CEO to the newest employee wants to be part of an organization that looks out for one another. Good attitudes, interpersonal interaction, and a pervasive positive spirit results from genuine renewal. Routines no longer seem so ordinary, and challenges are met with optimism. Renewing an organization goes deeper than processes and procedures. It must also include the renewing of relationships, the building of corporate morale, and the strengthening of interpersonal cooperation and commitment.

CONCLUSION
RE
JOICE!

I wake up every morning with a great desire to live joyfully.
—Alexandra Stoddard

"Leaders. They manage themselves, inspire others, and forge the future. They are full of questions and wary of easy answers. They explore and dream and are tireless believers in people. They are willing to take risks and are committed to excellence—along with readiness, virtue, and vision. Leaders strive to face things as they are and prepare for things as they will be."[1]

Elton Trueblood, the Quaker theologian, wrote, "We have made at least a start in discovering the meaning in human life when we plant shade trees under which we know full well we will never sit."[2] Leadership in its fullest and finest expression is not about today or even tomorrow—it is about next year and ten years from now and beyond. John Wesley said that the God who took care of the universe before he was born would surely care for it when he was gone; Wesley's job was to improve the present moment.

LEADERSHIP: A MARATHON

Every four years the eyes of the world are fixed on a gleaming new national stadium in the heart of some city, Beijing in 2008, London in 2012, as hundreds of athletes from around the globe, men and women of nearly every tribe and nation, enter the arena for a majestic opening ceremony of the Summer Olympics. It is a magnificent, rousing event as the pageantry and ritual of this worldwide gathering are beamed to billions of people via satellite.

It is a truly stirring moment; but it is not the most stirring moment of the Olympic Games. You see, it is not how one starts the race that really matters. It is how one finishes that determines defeat or victory. Therefore, one of the most dramatic moments of the Olympic Games will be the end of the marathon. The running of the Olympic marathon goes back to the very beginning days of the Olympics in ancient Greece. It mirrors a famous event that took place during a pivotal battle between the armies of Greece and Persia.

The soldiers were locked in mortal combat just outside a Grecian city named Marathon. Since the future of Greece hung in the balance, thousands waited anxiously in Athens to hear the news of the battle. Near the end of the day, the people of the city spotted a lone runner cresting a hill at the edge of town. He had run the entire distance from Marathon to Athens—well over twenty-five miles—without stopping. As he burst through the gates of the city, he lifted his head and cried forth one word—"Victory!" It is the Olympic marathon that links the modern games to ancient Greece. The official distance of the race is twenty-six miles, three hundred eighty-five yards.

For me, the end of the marathon is always a highlight moment of the Olympic Games as the athletes enter the stadium at the end of a grueling, joyful run. However, what I like most is that the crowd doesn't cheer just for the winner. Have you noticed that about a marathon? As each individual enters the stadium, a new round of applause breaks forth as each runner finishes.

There are eight hundred "official" marathons each year worldwide, such as the Boston, Chicago, New York, and so on. Ninety-nine and nine-tenths percent of the people who run in marathons do not run to win—they run to finish. A marathon is not so much a competition as it is an accomplishment. Leadership in the same place over a long period of time is a marathon, and just like the race, it is not how one starts the race that really matters. It is *how* one finishes.

THE MERCHANT OF DEATH

Alfred Nobel dropped the newspaper and put his head in his hands. It was 1888. Alfred was a Swedish chemist who made his fortune inventing and producing dynamite. His brother, Ludwig, had died in France. But Alfred's grief was compounded by dismay, for he had just read an obituary in a French newspaper—not his brother's obituary but his. An editor had confused the brothers. The headline read, "The Merchant of Death Is Dead."

This obituary described a man who had gotten rich by helping people kill one another. Shaken by this appraisal of his life, Nobel resolved to use his wealth to change his legacy. When he died eight years later, he left his estate to fund awards for people whose work benefited humanity. The awards, of course, became known as the Nobel Prizes.

Alfred Nobel had a rare opportunity—to look at the assessment of his life at its end, to read his own obituary, and still have the chance to change it. He decided to invest in something of lasting value, and his story has helped change the world and inspire men and women around the world. He actively began to change his image and determine his lasting legacy.

A LIFE OF GIVING

A popular bumper sticker reads, "He who dies with the most toys wins." What it does not say is that "He who dies with the most toys still dies." In that moment the measure of one's life will not be what he or she has in bank accounts, houses, lands, or toys; the true measure will be based on what the person did with what he or she had.

A couple of years ago a collection of artifacts from the grave of the ancient Egyptian king Tutankhamen was on display in Chicago at the Museum of Natural History. It is amazing to see all the treasure and other artifacts that were placed in King Tut's Tomb. He was certainly a young man who died with the most toys, but what did it matter?

I have been to Cairo and Upper Egypt, stood in the Valley of the Kings outside Luxor, and viewed the site of the tomb of King Tut.

But there is another tomb in Egypt that to me is more noteworthy. It is the grave of a young American named William Borden.

By the time Bill Borden graduated from a Chicago high school, as heir to the Borden Dairy estate, he was already a millionaire. For his high school graduation present, his parents gave him a trip around the world.

He attended Yale University. During his college years, Bill Borden made one entry in his personal journal that defined who he was going to be and what he was going to do with his life. That entry said simply: "Say 'no' to self and 'yes' to Jesus every time."

From Yale he attended Princeton Seminary to prepare for a life of missionary service. When he finished his studies at Princeton, he left America for the mission field. Because he was hoping to work with Muslims, he stopped first in Egypt to study Arabic. Shortly after his arrival, he contracted spinal meningitis. Within a month, twenty-five-year-old William Borden was dead. Like young King Tut, his life had been cut short.

He was buried in Egypt, but his Bible was sent home along with his other belongings. In the flyleaf of that Bible he had written these words: "No reserves. No retreats. No regrets."

Not many people make their way to see Bill Borden's grave in Egypt; no museums display his things. But his life has served as an inspiration for many, and his inheritance was given to the work of missions. His story is a good story that reminds us that we make a living by what we get, but we build a life by what we give.

In the final analysis, leadership comes down to a life of giving. The directional arrows of a leader's life go outward rather than inward. For a leader, the questions are not "What do I get out of this?" or "How will this make me look?" The test of leadership, over time, is not to be measured in terms of how well the leader fared, how rich or highly regarded he or she became. The true test is a determination of how well the organization one leads does over time.

Leadership is not for the faint of heart. It is satisfying and frustrating at the same time. It is challenging and rewarding. The pressure is constant, and the weight of responsibility is heavy. However, leaders who can re-vision their work, their organization, and their life over long stretches of time are the men and women who leave a legacy. And they are the ones who in the midst of the challenges of leadership can rejoice.

NOTES

INTRODUCTION

1. David Neidert, *Four Seasons of Leadership* (Provo, Utah: Executive Excellence Publishing, 1999), 73.

CHAPTER 1

1. Howard Schultz, *Onward: How Starbucks Fought for Its Life Without Losing Its Soul* (New York: Rodale, 2011), 250.

2. "Leaving a One-of-a-Kind Legacy." *Sibley on Health,* spring 2012 (published by Sibley Memorial Hospital, Washington, D.C.), 1.

3. "Lessons Learned," address by Robert L. Sloan to The Interagency Institute for Federal Health Care Executives, April 20, 2012. Used by permission of Robert Sloan.

4. "Leaving a One-of-a-Kind Legacy," 2.

5. Schultz, *Onward,* 28.

6. Warren Bennis and Robert Townsend, *Reinventing Leadership: Strategies to Empower the Organization* (New York: HarperCollines, 1995), 45.

7. Ibid., 46.

8. Noel M. Tichy and Mary Anne Devanna, *The Transformational Leader* (New York: John Wiley & Sons, 1986), xii.

9. John C. Bowling, *Grace-Full Leadership* (Kansas City: Beacon Hill Press of Kansas City, 2000), 31.

10. Ibid., 32.

CHAPTER 2

1. Marshall Goldsmith, *What Got You Here Won't Get You There* (New York: Hyperlon Publishing, 2007).

2. Ibid., 15.

3. Goerge Keller, *Transforming a College: The Story of a Little-Known College's Strategic Climb to National Distinction* (Baltimore: The Johns Hopkins University Press, 2004), xiii.

4. Ibid., 4.

5. Ibid., 7.

6. Ibid., 9.

7. Ibid.

8. Tichy and DeVanna, *The Transformational Leader*, 111.

9. Goldsmith, *What Got You Here Won't Get You There*, 35.

10. Carmine Gallo, *The Innovation Secrets of Steve Jobs* (New York: McGraw Hill, 2011), 12.

11. Richard Bode, *First You Have to Row a Little Boat* (New York: Usmer Press, 1993), 13-14.

12. Goldsmith, *What Got You Here Won't Get You There*, 17.

13. Ibid., 19.

CHAPTER 3

1. Keller, *Transforming a College*, 16.

2. George Weigel, "Europe's Problem—and Ours," *First Things* 140 (February 2004), 21.

3. John Maxwell, *The 21 Irrefutable Laws of Leadership* (Nashville: Thomas Nelson Publishers, 1908), 21.

4. John G. Miller, *QBQ! The Question Behind the Question* (New York: G. Putnam's Sons, 2004), 7-8.

CHAPTER 4

1. Schultz, *Onward*, flyleaf.

2. Ibid., 23.

3. Ibid., 111.

4. Ibid., 25.

5. John Bowling, *Above All Else* (Kansas City: Beacon Hill Press of Kansas City, 2012), 63.

6. Neidert, *Four Seasons of Leadership*, 9.

7. Theodore Levitt, *Thinking About Management* (New York: The Free Press, 1991), 27.

CHAPTER 5

1. David McNally, *Even Eagles Need a Push: Learning to Soar in a Changing World* (New York: Delacorte Press, 1990), 2.

2. Information concerning this process is found at <http://www.bcwinstitute.com/>.

3. Schultz, *Onward*, 260.

4. Wayne Lambert, quoted in *The Olivetian*, Issue 2, 2012 (published by Olivet Nazarene University), 15.

5. Bill Joiner and Stephen Josephs, *Leadership Agility: Five Levels of Mastery for Anticipating and Initiating Change* (San Francisco: Jossey-Bass, 2007).

6. Ibid, 4.

7. Ibid., 6.

8. Ibid., 10.

9. Ibid. 11.

10. Ibid., 254.

11. John C. Bowling, *Making the Climb: What a Novice Learned about Life on Mt. Kilimanjaro* (Kansas City: Beacon Hill Press of Kansas City, 2006).

CHAPTER 6

1. McNally, *Even Eagles Need a Push*, 140.

2. Schultz, *Onward*, 253.

3. Goldsmith, *What Got You Here*, 43-44.

4. Ibid., 45.

5. Ibid., 52.

6. Ibid., 61.

7. Ibid., 86.

8. Ibid., 93.

9. <http://footnotessincethewilderness.wordpress.com/2010/07/29/george-washington-pardons-traitor-michael-widman/> and <http://www.sermonillustrations.com/a-z/l/love_of_enemies.htm>.

CHAPTER 7

1. John Kotter, "What Leaders Really Do," *Harvard Business Review on Leadership* (Cambridge, Mass: Harvard Business School Press, 1998), 38.

2. Ibid., 45.

3. Ibid. 46.

4. Michael J. Gelb and Tony Buzam, *Lessons from the Art of Juggling: How to Achieve Your Full Potential in Business, Learning and Life* (New York: Harmony BOoks, 1994).

5. Ibid., xiii.

6. Tim O'Brien, *The Things They Carried* (New York: Houghton Mifflin, 1990), 1.

7. Ibid., 2.

8. Ibid., 3.

9. Ibid.

10. Gelb, *Lessons from the Art of Juggling*, 81.

CHAPTER 8

1. Nicholas Lemann, "Transaction Man: Mormonism, Private Equity, and the Making of a Candidate" in *The New Yorker*, October 1, 2012, 46.

2. Ibid.

3. John Kotter, *Leading Change* (Boston: Harvard Business School Press, 1996), 124-27.

4. Ibid., 125.

5. Ibid., 126.

6. Keller, *Transforming a College*, 102.

7. Ibid., 103.

8. Daniel H. Burnham, <http://thinkexist.com/quotes/daniel_h._burnham/>.

9. Edward M. Hallowell, *The Human moment at Work*, reprinted in *Harvard Business Review on Bringing Your Whole Self to Work* (Cambridge, Mass.: Harvard Business School Publishing, 2008). 23ff.

10. Ibid., 25.

11. Ibid., 26.

12. Ibid., 39.

CHAPTER 9

1. Tichy and Devanna, *The Transformational Leader*, 4.

2. Ibid., 28.

3. <http://www.bereanpublishers.com/Favorite_Stories/easy_eddie_and_his _son.htm>.

4. Ibid.

CHAPTER 10

1. Bennis and Townsend, *Reinventing Leadership*, 29.

2. <http://adage.com/article/special-report-the-advertising-century/ad-age -advertising-century-top-10-slogans/140156/>.

3. Philip W. Eaton, *Engaging the Culture, Changing the World* (Downers Grove, Ill:, Intervarsity Press, 2011), 42.

4. Ibid., 40, 42

5. Tichy and Devanna, *The Transformational Leader*, 122.

6. Gallo, *The Innovation Secrets of Steve Jobs*, 31.

7. Ibid., 10-11.

8. Stanford University, "You've Got to Find What You Love," Stanford Report, June 14, 2005, <http://news.stanford.edu/news/2005/june15/grad -061505.html?view=print>.

9. Daniel Morrow, "Excerpts from an Oral History Interview with Steve Jobs," Smithsonian Institution (oral and video histories), April 20, 1995, <http:// americanhistory.si.edu/collections/comphist/sj1.html>, (site discontinued).

10. Gallo, *The Innovation Secrets of Steve Jobs*, 41.

11. Computer History Museum, "The Computer History Museum Makes Historic Apple Documents Available to the Public," press release, June 2, 2009, <computerhistory.org/press/Apple-IPO-and-Macintosh-Plans.html>.

12. Gallo, *The Innovation Secrets of Steve Jobs*, 87.

13. Ibid., 155.

14. Ibid., 201.

CHAPTER 11

1. Bennis and Townsend, *Reinventing Leadership*, 1.

2. Gary Kelly, "Happy 40th Birthday!" *Spirit* magazine, June 2011 (published by Southwest Airlines, Dallas), 12.

3. Herb Kelleher, "We Owe It All to You" in *Spirit* magazine, June 2011 (published by Southwest Airlines, Dallas), 22.

4. "40 Lessons to Learn from Southwest," *Spirit* magazine, June 2011, 82 ff.

5. <http://www.kirupa.com/forum/archive/index.php/t-167788.html>.

6. <http://www.kirupa.com/forum/archive/index.php/t-167788.html>.

7. Warren Bennis, *An Invented Life* (Reading, Mass.: Addison-Wesley Publishing Company, 1993), xiii

8. Ibid., 1-2.

9. <http://thinkexist.com/quotation/never_look_down_to_test_the_ground _before_taking/13092.html>.

CHAPTER 12

1. Robert Coles, *Harvard Diary: Reflections on the Sacred and the Secular* (New York: The Crossroads Publishing Company, 1988), 111.

2. Ibid.

3. William Shakespeare, *Hamlet*, Act 1, Scene 3. Polonius is speaking to his son Laertes.

CONCLUSION

1. Bennis and Townsend, *Reinventing Leadership*, 153.

2. Neidert, *Four Seasons of Leadership*, 18.

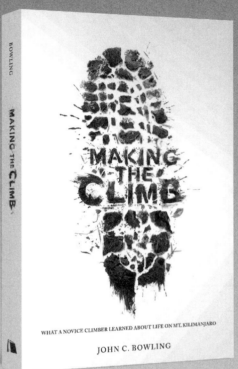

View leadership through the lens of grace.

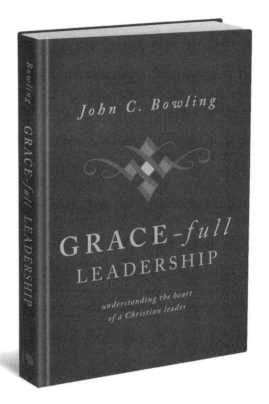

God has redefined the world of management for the Christian leader through scripture. In *Grace-Full Leadership*, Bowling explores the leadership qualities and practices that are distinct within the community of Christian leadership. Discover how to become a leader who generates exponential growth in spiritual gains—an eternity of difference from today's capital gains.

Grace-Full Leadership
Understanding the Heart of a Christian Leader
By John C. Bowling
ISBN 978-0-8341-2602-2
$17.99 (Hardcover)

www.BeaconHillBooks.com

BEACON HILL PRESS
OF KANSAS CITY